SUPER SQUAD

The 60s and 70s greats who transformed English football

Best wishes

Colin White

SUPER SQUAD

The 60s and 70s greats who
transformed English football

COLIN WHELAN

Troubador Publishing Ltd
Unit E2 Airfield Business Park,
Harrison Road, Market Harborough,
Leicestershire LE16 7UL
Tel: 0116 279 2299
Email: books@troubador.co.uk
Web: www.troubador.co.uk

ISBN 978-1-83628-161-0

British Library Cataloguing in Publication Data.
A catalogue record for this book is available from the British Library.

Printed and bound in Great Britain by 4edge Limited
Typeset in 11pt Garamond Pro by Troubador Publishing Ltd, Leicester, UK

This book is dedicated to Huntingdon

Contents

Acknowledgements

To my wife, Anne, for giving me a lend of her laptop; and for providing insight into the world of publishing. And for sporting the typos.

To my mum and dad for raising me as a child, who loved his football; and for indulging my child-like inconsistencies, by buying me 'Georgie Best Slippers' and an Arsenal shirt with a No.10 on the back, to go with the slippers.

To Edward Lishak for inventing the magnificently entertaining Facebook site 'Football in the 60s and 70s'; and to one of the site's great contributors, Neil Sambrook, for all his encouraging words.

To all my great mates, who encouraged me with the words "Give it a go!"And my 'Boxing Rebels' family.

To anyone I have ever accosted, stuck my phone in front of their face and said "Ere yar – read that". I apologise, but I thought you said you liked football, and I thought you might like to read one of the chapters I had just written. But I thank you for reading it anyway.

Introduction

There is a total truth to be had for most of our generation of football fans: we absolutely despise the game of football, as it exists today.

We hate VAR; we don't understand why players earn so much; we don't understand how a tussle for a ball can leave two players on the ground, choking for breath; we don't understand why everyone sits down at a game now; and we don't like our pundits yapping and stating the 'bleedin' obvious'.

But we still watch it.

We still love it – we don't despise it. We still buy the 'Sky Package'. We still go and blow 30 or 40 quid down the pub on a Sunday afternoon, just to watch it.

And the reason our generation still loves football – with some hardened individuals still attending matches – is because we had the greatest grounding you could ever wish for, if you chose football as your sport to follow.

Our generation (born between 1940-70) witnessed the absolute peak of English football, roughly between the years of 1960-79. We saw the two greatest-ever English players; the two greatest-ever Scottish players; and we saw George Best. And he was better than all of them.

We witnessed the emergence of a new breed of managers, too – managers with a personality. The likes of Allison, Clough, Docherty, Nicholson, Revie, Shankly and Paisley soon came to dominate English football, not just with their successes, but also with their presence on our TV screens. And we saw the re-emergence of a great manager, from his own dark tragedy of the 50s: Sir Matt Busby, perhaps the very best of them all.

This book seeks to tell the story of this glorious era through the careers of [a squad] 23 players, who, I believe, had the greatest impact on English football during this time; and how their influence laid a path for football as it is today.

But this isn't just the story of our very best players. This is also the story of those players we may not have noticed, those we mocked unfairly, those we may have forgotten. For those players left their own lasting legacy on the game, and this book seeks to honour that legacy.

The book also touches upon the other three great influences on English football at this time: the abolition of the maximum wage in 1961; the emergence of television; and the, separate, emergence of colour television. Before television, we relied on *Pathe Newsreels* and newspapers to tell us the story of football in this country; or fans had to attend in person, to catch a glimpse of the heroes they had maybe first encountered in a football annual.

By the way, if you think that the emergence of 'television' and 'colour television' are one and the same, just ask anyone from our vintage generation about the first FA Cup Final they watched on a colour telly. Try not to be too stunned, by a recall that is both instant and magnificent in its detail. Colour TV was a game-changer, alright.

I lived through most of this era, as I was born in 1963. I remember always wanting to know more about the game.

And I always loved football. It was always there; I always watched it. I played in the school team, too.

My mum and dad totally indulged that passion, too, to their great credit. I even watched the 1974 World Cup Final on a portable telly, hooked up to my dad's car battery. The family had planned an afternoon out, to nearby Grafham Water (a big field, a big lake and an ice cream van), and because I was only 10, I couldn't be left at home by myself. So, the portable telly and my dad's car battery were the compromise, just so that I didn't spend the next year whining.

I read all the glossy, colour magazines, all the 'annuals'. I loved the whole spectacle of it, once going a whole season, 1973-74, only missing one Match of the Day. I wasn't devoted in that way that I had to be at a match; and I freely admit that I was wanton in my choices of team, who I would support. Even now, at the age of 60, piss is extracted because I have a list of about three or four teams I "sometimes" support. I class myself as a "massive fan of football" – I am happy with that description.

But from the age of around eight, I also became a little geeky about football, and sport in general. And it has stuck with me, ever since. Yes, I do know that Jeff Astle scored in extra time, as West Brom beat Everton 1-0 in the 1968 FA Cup Final. I didn't watch the game, but it's just there because I looked it up once. And it'll probably never go away.

That geekiness doesn't hide my love for football, however. I'm not just that 'Rain Man' to be wheeled out in pubs, who sits there, and answers questions being fired at him about football – although, I'm not saying that hasn't happened. But anyone who knows me knows that football is my No.1 sport, the sport I love the most.

And just to add to my undying wonder of this era in football, I came across a Facebook site, during the first Covid lockdown, 'Football in the 60s and 70s'. I soon discovered that it was an incredibly entertaining site, populated by very passionate and knowledgeable fans, worldwide.

I totally fell in love with the site, and was soon sharing my own memories of this great era. And because a passion had been rekindled, I started to read about all the other stuff I had missed in the earlier part of the 60s. The Spurs 'Double' winning team; Man United's rebuild, post-Munich; the very sudden emergence of Leeds – all hugely fascinating stuff to me.

And, like you might do, I decided to write a book, which would incorporate many of those events.

Some may find some of the content in the book a bit gushy – too hagiographic in nature – for which I make few apologies. The chapters are affectionate portraits of my heroes, who all played football in the English First Division when I was a kid, or just before. Amazingly, some of the players I have written about became my newer heroes, after I discovered more about them in my 50s. And the players I have included in this book, are, in many ways, pioneers – they all moved the game forward.

There's still a world of wonder out there, whenever I delve back into my childhood memories of football. To this day, my very favourite colour combination is the yellow and blue that Arsenal wore in the 1971 FA Cup Final; the first Cup Final I watched on a colour telly. I still get very emotional when I watch a recording of the 1966 World Cup Final – a game I didn't see live. And I still lament the end of Mick Jones' career at Leeds with a knee injury, 50 years ago.

I'm just hoping that I have shared enough of these great memories in an engaging, passionate and accurate way, so that others might feel just a bit of what it was like for me to write this book.

"Whether you're a player, manager, trainer, director, supporter, reporter, kit man or tea lady, football possesses the power to make the week ahead sparkle with a sense of joyous well-being, or black with the unpalatability of unrealised hope and expectation."

Danny Blanchflower

Viv Anderson

The first black footballer to win a full cap for England

"Viv Anderson has pissed a fatness test"
John Helm, Yorkshire TV

And he would now, even at the age at 68. In fact, there was never a strip of fat on the elegant and long-legged right-back – "Spider" – who turned out with such distinction for Nottingham Forest, Arsenal. Manchester United and Sheffield Wednesday, between 1975–1993. There was also the small matter of playing for England 30 times. By doing so, he became the first black player to earn a full cap for England, in 1978 against Czechoslovakia.

"Sheffield United unearth hidden treasure on Bridlington Beach" would have made some headline back in the early 70s. And although Viv Anderson was, indeed, spotted as a schoolboy by a scout, playing alone with a ball on that very beach, the course of his early career didn't quite match the fictional, prescient headline. Anderson was actually noticed by a Manchester United scout at that trial for Sheffield United, and there then followed a year spent travelling to and from Manchester, trying to gain his apprenticeship. Sadly, he was rejected – cue the heartbreak of a rejected apprentice.

As luck and talent would have it, however, three weeks after Man United had rejected him, Anderson won an apprenticeship at Nottingham Forest. Viv's 'luck' snowballed from there: youth team at 17, and then the arrival of Brian Clough, as a manager in 1975. Clough, and Peter Taylor, recognised that talent and made Anderson a regular part of the team that won promotion to Division 1 in 1977.

And it was Clough – no surprise there – who acted as the catalyst for the take-off of Anderson's career. The 19-year-old Anderson had been pelted with bananas and other fruit during a warm-up against Carlisle in the mid-1970s – as we all know, this was not an uncommon experience for black players at that time. Understandably, a young, isolated and fearful black footballer sought out his manager for a shoulder to cry on, someone to recognise and sympathise with his plight.

Clough was having none of it, however, telling Viv to "Go back out there and get me two pears and a banana." He also told him "You let people like that dictate to you, you're not going to make it as a footballer". At that point, Viv Anderson made a conscious decision to just dismiss it and concentrate on his football. It was to be the bravest and most rewarding decision of his life.

We all know what happened next, as the unheralded, slumbering nobodies from the East Midlands, started to win trophies galore. Between 1978 and 1980, Nottingham Forest won a First Division Championship; two League Cups; two European Cups and one European Super Cup. Before that, Forest had only ever won two FA Cups, and one of those had been in 1898! And the very quick right-back, who could tackle a bit, made more than his fair contribution to this outstanding success.

As well as lifting the league title, becoming only the fifth promoted side to win the championship at the first attempt. Forest also won the Football League Cup that season. They conceded just 24 goals, scoring 69. They were seven points ahead of Liverpool in second place.

But it was the magic wand that Clough and Taylor wielded, that transformed bang average players from Division 2 journeymen into European Cup winners. That's what set them apart from the other managerial partnerships. The past-it players, the out-of-shape misfits – they were all welcome. And even the ones who just lingered in the background, but were prepared to work hard and showed immense strength of character – they could become England right-backs, too.

Forest gradually declined, of course. They didn't win another, proper, trophy until their 1989 League Cup win over Luton. Anderson left for Arsenal in 1984, guiding the younger players in the squad, and winning a League Cup winners' medal in 1987; he was also chosen for the 1986-87 PFA Team of the Season.

He then became Alex Ferguson's first signing at Manchester United, staying with them for three seasons, and picking up a Charity Shield winners' medal in 1990. Viv then enjoyed a swansong at Sheffield Wednesday, after his free transfer from Manchester United in 1991, helping them to promotion to Division 1 and to third in the same league, the season after.

During his club playing career, Viv Anderson played for Brian Clough; Alex Ferguson; George Graham; and Ron Atkinson, among others. That is some roll-call.

As for his England career, it somewhat disappointed after the fanfare of his arrival into the team in 1978. Even though Anderson did enjoy a 30-cap, 10-year career for his national team, he never nailed down a place as a regular starter. He played one game in the 1980 European Championships, and although part of the next two World Cup squads in 1982 and 1986, he didn't taste one minute of action.

Around that time, of course, England were blessed with quality right backs, with Phil Neal and Mick Mills marginally preferred ahead of Anderson. And by the time of the 1986 World Cup, Everton's Gary Stevens had won a place ahead of Anderson in the First XI. Stevens took a bit of criticism at that World Cup, particularly after England's exit to Argentina, but he still held sway by the time England left for Germany to contest the 1988 Euros. So much sway, in fact, that yet again, England's reserve right-back, Anderson, didn't get a look in. That's some unwelcome record: four international tournaments, and only one game played.

Viv Anderson enjoyed a great football career. There's a tinge of disappointment that his England career didn't match the achievements of his club career. But does any footballer get out of the game without their own share of regret? You'd doubt it.

He was also a pioneer, a 'first'. He was the first black football player to win a full international cap for England. But also, just as importantly, Viv Anderson won two European Cup winners' medals and a First Division winner's medal. And for a while, he was the best right-back in England.

He was just a very, very good footballer.

Alan Ball

The commodity

"Young man, you will never play a better game in your life."

Sir Alf Ramsey, following the
1966 World Cup final

Alan Ball is a great fit for this era, his peak perfectly straddling our two decades. A World Cup winner at 21, he played well into his 30s and still won a League Cup runners-up medal for Southampton in 1979, at the age of 34. He was the outstanding player in England for a period, probably 1968-71. His vision, awareness, one-touch and quick feet, the beacon within an already gifted Everton team.

It was at Blackpool, where it all began for Alan Ball. His dad, Alan Ball, Senior, had conned the directors into giving his boy a trial, after the likes of Bolton and Wolves had already turned him down for being too small. He impressed enough to stay with the club for four years, and earn 12 England caps.

In truth, the 'big clubs' had been circling Blackpool well before the World Cup, but once the whole world had seen England's little gem run the show in the final, Blackpool wouldn't stand a chance of keeping him. FA Cup winner's

Everton swooped in, to take the 21-year-old to Goodison Park for a record £110,000 fee.

And Everton suited Alan Ball so very well. He fitted into the perfectly-balanced midfield, with Kendall and Harvey, described by many as the greatest English midfield ever, up until that time. But Ball was still the standout of the three, with his competitiveness and relentless running. He was always that one player who would be available to a team-mate, never hiding.

A losing cup-finalist in 1968, and then a League Championship winner in 1970, everything was moving in the right direction for Ball and Everton – they were looking a formidable force for years to come. However, a sudden tailing-off of form meant that Everton would only finish 14th the season after their title triumph, winning only 12 league games all season.

It is often said that the decline of Everton began immediately after the return of the 1970 England World Cup squad, as Everton had contributed three outfield players to the starting XI. The searing heat of Mexico, the playing of games of football in the midday sun, were not the norm for Labone, Newton and Ball. That longer recovery time hurt Everton's momentum going into the next season, more than other teams who had contributed fewer players.

But it was the season after that, where Everton effectively threw in the towel: they let Alan Ball go. They let their best player – England's best player – be transferred to another Division 1 team.

And it's this piece of business, where you might realise for the first time, that one of your footballing heroes was nothing but a commodity to be traded – just like gold, tea, and wheat – if the price were right. It didn't matter how 'special' your favourite player was to you. That player might well have been the very reason why you started supporting your team – but you soon discovered that he could just as easily be got rid of by your club, if they thought they could get good money for him.

So, in December 1971, it played out thus: Alan Ball was summonsed to Harry Catterick's office and informed that Everton, his club, wanted rid of him, because Arsenal were prepared to pay £220,000 for his services.

Despite Ball's impassioned protests that he didn't want to leave, an unrepentant Catterick responded "I've had you for five years. I am making a profit on you, and I have had an awful lot out of you. Football's a business, son".

And didn't we now know it.

Alan Ball did well for Arsenal – they got their five years, too. But he did well out of Arsenal as well. A 10% signing on fee, a pay packet of £250 per week. That package to entice Alan Ball to Highbury drew some of the sting from his emotional departure away from Goodison. That worked both ways, however.

Bertie Mee soon had another battle on his hands, once news of that pay package leaked, and the likes of "90-quid-a-week-double-winning-scorer" Charlie George found out. The maximum wage had only been abolished in football ten years previously, of course, and clubs were now being confronted by the first signs of 'player power'.

Ball didn't win another top-level trophy in his career, but he played in another Cup Final, and Arsenal finished second in the league in 1972-73, just faltering away at the last. Ball was also there, preparing the way, as the next great generation of Arsenal greats came through: Brady; O'Leary; and Stapleton. But he was on his way by the end of 1976.

He then saw out his club career via two spells at Southampton and two stints in the NASL; he even managed a one season player-managerial stint at his first love Blackpool in the early 80s.

Alan Ball's England career never quite matched those herculean efforts on the pitch in 1966. He ran Karl-Heinz Schellinger ragged that day, an easy pick for 'Man of the Match'. His actual tournament had, initially, promised to be one huge anti-climax, as Ramsey had dropped him after the 0-0 draw with Uruguay. But of the four players that Ramsey dropped during the tournament (the others were Paine; Connelly; and Callaghan) only Ball would earn a recall. England's own Tinkerman from 1966 did finally find a way.

His England career was ended by one of the many decisions made by Don Revie that never quite made sense. Ball had been Revie's captain for the previous six games and then, without explanation, he dropped Ball from further international duty. A letter sent from the FA, acted as a mere follow-up to a journalist calling Alan's wife, to break the news that Revie had dropped Alan. And he sold that World Cup Winners' medal ("just a lump of gold") in 2004, so that his family could enjoy financial security.

You do pick up and you do remember some of the things said about Alan Ball, even towards the end of his career. Because even at the end of his career, Kevin Keegan said that he'd won the European Footballer of the Year award twice, but he learned something new every day in training from Alan Ball at Southampton. You read even now, that the players who played with and against him, name Alan Ball as their favourite player. He was just that good.

The leaving of Everton spelt heartbreak for Evertonians: their greatest-ever player treated as no more than a commodity. It spelt heartbreak for Alan Ball, too. He didn't leave on good terms. But the fans and the club, they still love, they still idolise their Alan Ball.

A truly great football player.

Gordon Banks

The first modern keeper

"Of all the players to lose, we had to lose him"
Sir Alf Ramsey

It is the great privilege – and the great risk – for those that play at an international level, that a career and legacy can be established, or ruined, within the space of a week. Geoff Hurst and Alan Ball in 1966; Bryan Robson in 1982; Gary Lineker in 1986, all announced their presence to the world at their respective world cups. Their physical presence in these games, provided the launch pad for their long and established international careers.

But with Gordon Banks, we observed something slightly different: the save from Pele at Mexico '70, proved his prowess forever. The sprint across the goal-line, to paw away a goal-bound header from the world's greatest footballer was extraordinary in its execution. But, more importantly, it was the game that he didn't play, the following Sunday, when we realised that it was his physical presence that England just could not do without. It was this realisation that truly cemented his legacy, coming so soon after that save. Bank's replacement that fateful Sunday afternoon in Leon, Peter Bonetti, also cemented his own legacy – a ruined one, sadly.

A product of Chesterfield's 'goalkeeping nursery', that has produced the likes of Wilson, Stevenson, Ogrizovic and Seaman over the years, Gordon Banks started his career with Chesterfield in 1953. He broke through into the first-team in 1958, before being snapped up by First Division Leicester City for the start of the 1959-60 season. He played in four cup finals for the club, as they were beaten in the 1961 and 1963 FA Cup finals, before winning the League Cup in 1964 and beaten finalists in 1965. By 1963, he had won his first cap for England, the first of his 73 appearances.

Typical of the regard in which goalkeepers were held at the time, Banks didn't have a goalkeeping coach, to share insight and experience. Instead, Banks had to hone his own skills, by devising drills and routines, and strengthening his perceived weaknesses, to improve his all-round game. The basics of the modern 'keeper were all there, though: instinct, great physical strength, athleticism, and excellent shot-stopping abilities. Standing at just 6 feet tall, you might only subtract 'overwhelming physical stature' from the full complement of the modern 'keeper.

So that by the time England were ready to host the 1966 World Cup, Gordon Banks had no real challengers for his position in the team. Stepney and Springett were there as back-up, should the unimaginable occur, but Banks would always be first choice. Six games and four clean sheets later, Gordon Banks was a World Cup winner, the rock at the last line of defence.

And, yet, strangely enough, a season after winning a World Cup Winners' medal, Banks's own club, Leicester City, thought that they had unearthed their own local gem as a replacement for Banks. Leicester thought so much of their protege, 18-year-old Peter Shilton, and so little of their world cup winner, that they were prepared to let Banks go to Stoke City for £52,500. No matter that the 'old man' at 29 was reaching his peak, and had much to pass onto the teenager, Leicester wanted a newer, younger replacement.

As events transpired, *Schadenfreude* rested its own hand upon Leicester City's shoulder, post-1967. Banks went on to win a second League Cup winners' medal in 1972, and the FWA Footballer of the Year award in the same year. Shilton learnt his apprenticeship at Leicester, without the guiding hand of Banks, and suffered relegation in the 1968-69 season. Shilton won nothing with Leicester, except a faux-Charity Shield winners' medal in 1971. Shilton was eventually sold to Stoke in 1974. It would take Brian Clough, Nottingham Forest and Shilton coming into his own peak in his late-20s, before he established a world-class reputation and made the England No.1 jersey his own.

As for Gordon's England career, it followed an upward trajectory. He was reaching the peak that is exclusively reserved for goalkeepers in their early to mid-30s, with a series of 'world's best' performances for his country. Indeed, Banks was chosen as FIFA Goalkeeper of the Year, in consecutive years between 1966–71. England's chances of winning a second World Cup at the forthcoming 1970 edition in Mexico, were now considerably enhanced by fielding the best goalkeeper in the world.

England's progression through Group C at the 1970 World Cup can be easily marked off as 'routine'. A 1–0 reversal to eventual winners and *Team of the Century*, Brazil, was sandwiched between comfortable 1-0 victories over Rumania and Czechoslovakia. And there was enough in the defeat to Brazil to offer encouragement to Alf Ramsey, that if in the very real possibility that the two teams should meet again in the final, England would prevail.

England's opponents in the quarter-final would be West Germany, the team they had beaten in '66, and a team that had only ever beaten England once. In a friendly – not in a competitive game of football. Again, progression to the next round was looking 'routine'.

It's not entirely known how a bug took over Gordon Bank's body on the eve of the game against West Germany, but it briefly infested his insides to the extent that expulsion occurred at both ends, as his body fought its own losing battle readying itself for Beckenbauer and co. A rudimentary 'fitness test' was passed, as England's management team fought desperately to get Banks onto the field of play for the next day. Shortly after, Banks returned to his room and collapsed.

Peter Bonetti – the reserve goalkeeper, who hadn't played a competitive game for six weeks, and who had struggled in training with the flight of the ball in the rarefied air of Mexico – replaced Banks, and made three mistakes as England crashed out of the 1970 World Cup. England lost 3-2 after leading 2-0, with 20 minutes to play.

Was it the water, was it the single beer Banks had drunk 48 hours before the game? Banks never knew; no one did. There was a charge thrown at Ramsey, that he should have taken greater care of his prime asset. But how much care could feasibly be expended towards Banks? Or Charlton, or Moore, or Ball? These guys were 'prime assets', too. But that afternoon in Leon showed us – something that we knew anyway – that Gordon Banks was absolutely irreplaceable.

Banks prolonged his peak, post-World Cup – he was still irreplaceable. A stellar display in both the 1972 League Cup Final and semi-final, won him his final domestic honours in football. But on a Sunday afternoon, in October 1972, as he drove home from a session on the treatment table at Stoke's Victoria Ground, Banks overtook a lorry and collided with a vehicle coming the other way. He suffered serious head injuries and was blinded in his right eye. He made an almost full recovery; but there was now no way he could play competitive football. England had lost its greatest ever goalkeeper.

However, in 1977, he made a comeback in the new and exciting North American Soccer League, with Fort Lauderdale Strikers. The NASL had a more liberal interpretation of the ruling that all goalkeepers should possess two fully functioning eyes, as Banks helped Fort Lauderdale to win the title in his first season there, conceding only 29 goals in 26 games.

He was voted the league's top goalkeeper of the season – not bad going at 40. Banks played another 11 games in the 1978 season, before finally retiring altogether from football.

Commanding, heroic, dominating – and there are so many more superlatives you could list about Gordon Banks. He was the best, the greatest – "the one we couldn't do without". He set the template for future goalkeepers everywhere, with his extra training and his sheer athleticism.

He was England's greatest-ever goalkeeper, above all else.

Colin Bell

Football's first "athlete"

"Colin was a lovely, humble man. He was a huge star for Manchester City, but you would never have known it"

Great friend, Mike Summerbee

There's a common accusation thrown at modern football, that the players these days are just big, strong athletes, who can run all day. Casting aside that isn't all they can do, or else they wouldn't actually be any good at playing the game of football, you might sometimes think "How did this all happen? How did the game evolve to the point where the skilful dribbler; the imposing, but static centre-half; the battering-ram up front, had been out-muscled and out-ran from the game?"

And you would do a lot worse than look to Colin Bell, to find your answer.

During a period between 1966 and 1975, we watched a type of footballer in English football we had never seen before. He was a player of incredible athleticism, combined with seemingly limitless stamina. Colin Bell wasn't tricky or very fast, but he just ran with the ball – constantly. He just wore the other midfield down because they couldn't physically keep up with him. For the first time, we were witnessing the results of an experiment, where the lungs of an 800-metre runner – or a racehorse called Nijinsky, if you prefer – were transplanted into the body of a supremely-skilled footballer. And the game would never be the same again.

Bell was signed by Manchester City from second division Bury in 1966, for £47,500, the boy of 19, captaining his team. Malcolm Allison had affected his best wide-boy persona to secure the transfer of Bell, reportedly attending a game at Gigg Lane, only to leave early, muttering – very loudly – "He can't pass and he can't tackle". City, supposedly, weren't interested, and plenty of other clubs were conned by the truth of that statement.

The Joe Mercer-Malcolm Allison managerial team at City had fashioned a decent side that had earned a respectable 15th place in the 1966-67 season, in their first season back in Division 1, after a three-year absence. After a few astute buys here and there, plus an impressive youth system, they found the one last piece of the jigsaw, when they bought Francis Lee from Bolton in 1967, for £60,000. With Lee, City had found their perfect balance and blend – they were now playing more aggressively and scoring more goals. They would now be challenging for honours.

And in the 1967-68 season, City won the league title for the first time in 31 years with Colin Bell inspirational throughout, earning him the 1967/68 Manchester City Player of the Year award. He was soon the most important player in the team, the absolute focal point. That City team won every domestic trophy in a three-year period between 1968 and 1970, and threw in a European Cup Winners'

Cup, for good measure. Bell was contributing around a goal every three games, as well as setting up goals for others. They would surely have won another league title in the 1971-72, too, but for Bell missing nine games towards the end of the season, as City lost the title to Derby County by one point.

But in that era where every club had their rock star player, Colin Bell was exactly not that. The undoubted star player in a City team of such competing talents, he preferred to blend into the background, spurn the accolades, and just get on with doing his job. Bell wasn't a wannabe rock star – he just wanted to crack on with his work. That he scored 142 goals in 481 games for City – just doing his job – is some record for a midfield player.

And then it happened. The world of Colin Bell came crashing down. And the world of English football came crashing down with it.

A Martin Buchan challenge in a League Cup match v Man United in November 1975, effectively finished Colin Bell's football career. It was a standard tackle that forwards would take in most matches back in 1975 e.g. just below the knee. But this time, Colin's right leg was anchored to the ground, which meant his knee took the full force of the tackle. With ligaments and cartilage torn, the whole leg was a grisly mess. The knee was a 'bag of blood', and he was fortunate that his leg wasn't amputated.

The rehabilitation process lasted over two years, culminating in a substitute's appearance at Maine Road on Boxing Day 1977, against Newcastle. Grown men were said to have wept, as Colin Bell took to the pitch, an ovation preceding him for a good four minutes.

But no matter.

Colin Bell's right knee may have been fit for everyday purposes, but, tragically, it was knackered for Division 1 football purposes. The engine was still there – a little slower to respond, maybe – but the complete flexion of the knee wasn't. This had a huge effect on the functioning of Colin's game. After a further 27 games over the next two seasons, Colin Bell left Maine Road. He then tried his luck in the US, with George Best and San Jose Earthquakes, but he only lasted five games.

Martin Buchan never said sorry for the tackle, nor did he visit Colin in hospital. But Colin Bell never blamed Buchan for that tackle.

Colin Bell's England career, it probably should be said, didn't quite reach the heights of his club career; he only scored nine goals in his 48 appearances. England, however, were a declining force, during the time of Bell's England career. But there is a popular misconception that needs to be challenged 50-odd years later.

Bell was the player brought on, to replace Bobby Charlton in the 1970 World Cup Quarter-Final v West Germany, when England were leading 2-1. The accepted narrative today is that "Charlton off, Bell on" led to England's capitulation and eventual defeat 3-2.

That isn't the case at all. England dominated extra-time in that game, with Bell at the heart of everything good that England did. He was even clattered by Beckenbauer – in front of the referee – in the penalty area. A penalty, however, was not awarded.

There were very good reasons why Bobby Charlton should have been taken off after 70 minutes in that Quarter-Final, but the introduction of Bell should in no way be blamed for England's defeat, heroic and undeserved as it was.

Colin Bell was a force of nature, the like of which, English football had never seen before. The shy, but confident young man, almost provided the antithesis of what star football players were in the 60s and 70s. He was nevertheless totally respected worldwide, for his fantastic footballing gifts and his Olympic athlete's engine.

And he has one of the greatest-ever football songs still sung about him, to this day.

(*To the tune of Yellow Submarine*):

"No.1 is Colin Bell, and No.2 is Colin Bell, and No.3 is Colin Bell, and No.4 is Bell as well..."

George Best

The Genius

"He was the first modern footballer – the one every mediocre millionaire of the modern game should get down on their knees and thank"

Jimmy Greaves

When it comes to writing a story of George Best, you could never quite do this fabulous football player justice. As much as we all loved watching him play, there is still so much we either did not see; or so much that we did see but that has been wiped from VT. We saw the development of the greatest football talent the UK has ever produced, and yet we didn't see the half of it.

We all know the origins of the story, of how George came over to Manchester, and how he failed to settle the first time, before returning to Belfast two days later. He did finally settle, however, making his debut for Manchester United in September 1963. Over the next eight years, his career built to such a peak, that George became UK football's greatest ever homegrown talent.

During this time, he won two First Division titles, a European Cup, Footballer of the Year and a Ballon d'Or. Tellingly, he had won the three major honours in club football by the age of 22. The great sadness, of course, was that from now on, his career would be a story of decline – relative at first, very swiftly followed by absolute.

As so many have explained over the years, it was Man United's inability to bring in international class signings to replace their ageing stars, that set back their winning cause after their European Cup win in 1968. Instead of kicking on from a position of strength, the club appeared to rest upon its laurels, glorying in their triumph at Wembley to partially compensate for the tragedy of Munich.

The club also suffered a destabilising mini 'managerial merry-go-round' between 1969 and 1972, with five holders of the post at various times. The burden of winning more trophies increasingly fell upon the one player approaching his peak, the one, who, overwhelmingly, was the best player in the First Division and Europe. Sadly, the guy couldn't do it alone; not without Crerand and Stiles, and not without the better versions of Law and Charlton.

The club did not manage the retirement of Sir Matt Busby at all well, and you wonder for the sake of George's career, would he have been better off seeking a new challenge elsewhere? We'll never know, but our greatest ever footballing talent should never have played all his greatest games, scored all his greatest goals, before the age of 26. The European Cup was the last honour George Best won in football – he had just turned 22.

The game of football George Best actually played seemed to be different to everyone else's. A dribbler – an insane dribbler – a scorer of incredible goals with both feet, a superb header of a ball for a smaller man, a brave and skilful tackler when called upon. George, genuinely, was that man who separated the viewer from their armchair, rising to their feet every time George received the ball. It mattered not, that the viewer would be watching recorded highlights and knew the result.

But it was that silky balance that really separated him from the rest. It was also the speed of that glide, whilst dribbling, that meant he was able to move away and ride tackles that would have otherwise inflicted terrible injury upon him.

That ability to evade the tackle/assault was God-given, of course, but it was also refined on the training ground at Carrington, where Crerand and Stiles would "aid" George's development. Not out of malice, but out of a genuine desire to help George's game, to toughen him up. Because at the same time George was toughening up, a lengthy queue had formed of opposition defenders wanting to cause physical harm to George's body. And it was during the 1971 League Cup Quarter Final, that George famously met the Ron Harris 'tackle' that never was, skipping over it, to round Bonetti and slot the ball into an empty net.

On the international stage, Northern Ireland were never quite good enough to qualify for World Cups or European Championships. But we were still treated to the occasional 'Best Cameo'. Kicking the ball, whilst in mid-air, perfectly legitimately, as Gordon Banks took a goal kick at Windsor Park in 1971. The goal was disallowed, of course. And the outrageous nutmeg of Johan Cruyff in 1976, as Northern Ireland drew 2-2 with Holland.

Away from football, the guy was also idolised by men of all ages, mostly, and adored by so many women. In the 60s – a different age, we all acknowledge that – he really was the best footballer in the country and probably the most handsome man in the country. Truly, an unbeatable combination! Feted everywhere, his earnings exploded, the sport's most marketable asset. He soon became a sports 'commodity' in this country, the first of his kind.

But where The Beatles and the Rolling Stones attracted and courted similar levels of attention, they were from the pop world; a world that had already learned to absorb and embrace the likes of Elvis. Their rise to cultural eminence was planned, and certainly more welcomed on their part.

But it was different for George – he played football, the people's game. Whilst we were used to seeing him most weeks on our TV screens – and gradually falling in love with him – it's doubtful that he wanted to become a cultural icon. He would much rather have just played football and entertained people, just enjoying his life. However, by accident, he did become exactly that. That level of pressure would exert its toll later in his career, as we all know.

As a nation, we were also fortunate to observe the metamorphosis of Georgie Best the boy, to George Best the man. We also watched this change during a television age that underwent its own transition from black and white to colour. George Best in that deep red Manchester United shirt became a genuine thing of beauty.

What George did after he left Manchester United is irrelevant in a footballing context, his best days, sadly, behind him. It was his presence, during his peak, 1963-1971, that lit up not just a sport, but a country. Among the outstanding competition from his fellow players, from competing arts genres, he was always the most skilled; the one many of us most aspired to. His influence and presence transforming the sport in a matter of years. TV, too, was coming of age; but it needed its screen stars to dazzle, for it to light up our living rooms in the 60s and 70s.

It was George Best's journey – part of his legacy – that played a huge part in this overall picture. He should never be forgotten for the part he played in this sudden and exciting cultural revolution.

And he will never be forgotten for being the greatest football player this country has ever produced.

Danny Blanchflower

Football's great intellectual

"People often ask me why I don't play as well for Ireland, as I do for Burnley. It's simple – Danny keeps me up all night talking"

Jimmy McIlroy, Northern Ireland and Burnley

There's no getting away from the fact that Danny Blanchflower could talk for Northern Ireland, as well as he could play football for Northern Ireland. There was a wonderful eloquence when the man spoke, a genuine passion and conviction, rolled into one. You could easily fill a whole chapter with 'The Quotes of D. Blanchflower'; and we would all be happy with our efforts, because he was *that* good with the words.

We heard his verbal eloquence away from the pitch, of course, in his many interviews both during and after his football career. TV producers soon learned that Danny Blanchflower was the 'go-to' player, when looking for a post-match interview, where they – and TV viewers – were often treated to a takeaway quote, or some great insight into the events on the pitch that day. And as events would gloriously coincide, Danny Blanchflower just happened to be captain of the greatest club team England had ever seen up until that point, the 1960-61 'Double Winners', Tottenham Hotspur.

But he wasn't just a great speaker. On the pitch, Blanchflower was known for his vision and movement in the midfield playmaking role. He had that crucial ability to dictate and change the tempo of a game. He was at least the equal of Mackay and White, the other two pieces of Spurs' midfield triumvirate, and he was the one who brought the extra guile and awareness to any team he played for.

Blanchflower started his career, playing for the Belfast team, Glentoran. But by 1949, he had come to England, to Barnsley, where he began a theme that would run right the way through his career. He fell out with manager Angus Seed and his training methods, because the team didn't practise with the ball as often as Danny might have liked. So, by 1951, he had moved to Aston Villa, where he made 155 appearances for the club, before making his career-defining move to Spurs in 1954 – a signing that would cost Spurs £30,000, the most expensive midfielder in Britain at the time.

Amazingly, given what he achieved at Spurs, he ran an almost constant, low-level squabble at the club. Manager Arthur Rowe had signed Danny, sharing the same ideals to the extent that the manager immediately wanted him to captain the team "He was a natural leader with the kind of commanding personality that compelled respect". However, Rowe resigned with ill health, a season later. This then preceded a damaging internal power-struggle, involving future England manager Alf Ramsey. The result of which led to first-team coach Jimmy Anderson taking over as manager.

He and Danny clashed on several occasions, most notably during the 1956 FA Cup semi-final against Birmingham, where the captain on the pitch assumed the role of the manager, pushing centre-half Maurice Norman upfield to join the forwards, as Spurs were trailing. That didn't work, and Danny was dropped for the next match. But, shortly after, the new manager would again resign through ill health.

Up until this time with Spurs, Danny was made and stripped of the captaincy twice, had a transfer request turned down, and had seen two managers retire with ill health. This was no football marriage made in heaven.

But when Bill Nicholson took over as manager in 1958, the penny began to drop for Blanchflower; even though he had been dropped earlier in the manager's first season. They reached an agreement on where the demarcation would lie between manager and the captain on the pitch – and once reinstated to the team, it was Danny Blanchflower who assumed the role as captain.

The improvement made in the 1959-60 season, carried on through to the following season, with Spurs winning their first 11 games. And the audacious claim that Danny had shared with his team-mates at the start of the season wasn't looking quite as fanciful now – the Double' was on. The league won at a canter, with Leicester brushed aside in the Cup Final.

The achievement of the 1961 'Double' winning side, should never be under-played. That feat hadn't been achieved for 64 years in English football. That's important context, when we consider that in the 63 years since, the Double has been accomplished on 10 separate occasions.

Spurs' achievement in 1961 was truly ground-breaking.

A season later, Danny captained Spurs to win the FA Cup against Burnley, a game in which he scored a penalty. The season after that he again captained Spurs to win the European Cup Winners' Cup – the first English team to win a European trophy. There was also the small matter of Danny winning the 1958 and 1961 FWA's Footballer of The Year award. Only eight other players have won the award twice, since its inception in 1948.

He also played 56 times for Northern Ireland, captaining the unfancied team to the World Cup quarter-finals in 1958. He was also chosen for FIFA World Cup All-Star Team in 1958. Only he could have lifted that team to such an elevated status.

Danny was also a thinker and an innovator. "He reckoned he invented the defensive wall because the Northern Ireland goalkeeper was so bad," his son Richard, once recalled. And he "invented" the passed penalty, long before Johan Cruyff. In a World Cup qualifier against Portugal in May 1957, he tapped it short to Jimmy McIlroy, who scored. The referee, inevitably, ordered the kick to be retaken, because everyone had to have a turn at disagreeing with Danny Blanchflower.

He also famously refused Eamonn Andrews' grand invitation to go on This Is Your Life. "I consider this programme to be an invasion of privacy. Nobody is going to press gang me into anything". The first person to refuse the invitation, the ground-breaker to a tee.

It seemed totally natural that Blanchflower would assume a managerial career, once his actual football career had finished; but it just never really happened. He did coach at Spurs for several years, and he did manage Northern

Ireland and Chelsea briefly in the 70s. His talents, however, were more drawn to commentary, punditry and writing.

Danny Blanchflower did actually make his unforgettable mark in two separate careers. A cultured, inspiring captain, who led the great Spurs side of the early-60s to the first 'Double' of the 20th Century. He then left an equally memorable legacy outside of football, with his eloquence and intellectual grasp, writing a hugely entertaining football column in the Daily Express. He stood up with the likes of Mackay and White, but he also deserves his place in the company of the likes of McIlvaney and Woolridge. A fantastically talented man in two separate careers.

The great, great tragedy is that Danny Blanchflower lost his life, at the early age of 67. And, in part, this was due to the ravages of Alzheimer's Disease, that cruel condition that just debilitates and makes a mockery of brain function.

And, probably, the greatest-ever brain in English football belonged to Danny Blanchflower.

"No play, movie or TV programme, work of literature, or music, induces such a polarisation of emotion on a weekly basis. We curse football for having this power" – Danny Blanchflower.

Billy Bremner

The manager's lieutenant

"Above all, Leeds have Bremner, the best footballer in the four countries. If every manager were given the choice of any one player to add to his team, some, no doubt, would toy with the idea of George Best; but the realists, to a man, would choose Bremner"

John Arlott

No, Bremner wasn't ever a better player than George Best. But for context, Best had only recently returned from a four-week ban for kicking the ball out of a referee's hands, and his shining star had just begun to fade with the footballing public.

But when John Arlott wrote those stirring words in April 1970, Billy Bremner was probably the dominant force in English football. His Leeds United stood on the cusp of an unprecedented treble, and it is no overstatement to say that it was Bremner's sheer will and drive that had taken Leeds to that cusp. The reality, however, is that the cusp was disguised as a precipice, as Leeds faltered at the very last.

In the space of 46 days, from 14 March onwards, Leeds played 15 fixtures, an average of three per week. These included two FA Cup finals, three semi-finals, two European

Cup semi-finals, one quarter-final and seven league games. Their efforts for fulfilling 63 fixtures that season, were rewarded with runners-ups in the League and FA Cup.

But Arlott's quote still stands as a worthy statement of where we were with English football in April 1970, and particularly with the contribution from its *Footballer of the Year Billy Bremner*.

There's no doubt William John Bremner divides opinion. To his detractors, he's the antithesis of what good football should be about, totally undermining his great talent by adopting a bullying persona, who did actually kick opponents. And elbow them and knee them and poke them – the embodiment of Revie's 'Dirty Leeds'. To his supporters, his talent was plain to see, bossing a game, controlling the flow, making the vital pass, not losing possession, winning the crucial games, with a goal out of nothing – but always displaying a deterring hint of violence.

But Billy Bremner's career would never have taken off the way it did, he may never have developed into the player he became, were it not for the influence, guidance and sheer nous of his second manager at Leeds, Don Revie. It was Revie who could see that Bremner's unselfishness and stamina may be better deployed in a central midfield role, rather than as a right winger. And it was Revie, who made the necessary tactical adjustments and who brought in the necessary supporting infrastructure – a Giles and a Collins – to get Leeds back into the First Division by 1964.

It was the meticulous preparation of 'The Don' that now reaped its rightful reward, as Leeds began to compete with the bigger clubs. Up until that point, Leeds were historically seen as a rugby league city, and had only ever won a Second Division title in 1924. Unheralded at the start of the 1964-65 campaign, they very nearly pulled off the heist of a League and Cup Double, losing the league on goal average to Manchester United, and losing the Cup Final to Liverpool in extra-time.

And that remarkable improvement would be found within the pages of Revie's 'dossiers', the notes he and his coaching staff had started to keep on Leeds' opponents. These notes outlined the key strengths and weaknesses of opposition players, ensuring that Leeds had the 'inside track' on how to compete and beat the opposition. A revolutionary concept of its time – often derided – it set the template for the video-analysis and stats breakdowns, used by today's coaches and managers.

But for the plan and the preparation to succeed, Revie would need a captain like Bremner out on the pitch – a lieutenant – to make any necessary in-play adjustments. Revie needed his reader to assess and adjust to what was required, and he needed a leader to communicate that new command to the troops. And those responsibilities lay with the one player Revie had learned to love and trust at Leeds.

And it was this relationship that was so crucial to Leeds success over the period; indeed, it was a relationship, the like of which we had not seen before. Almost unique within English football, the closest you might compare it to is the 'Ferguson-Keane axis', before the latter pair went their separate ways, citing "irreconcilable differences".

Billy Bremner went on to win every domestic honour in the game – and should have won those same honours a few more times. A captain to his adopted and beloved Leeds for 11 seasons. He played more than 50 games a season on eight occasions. He was the heartbeat of a great team, always diminished by his absence, he lived by his own motto "Side before self every time."

There is also much to be said for the idea that, despite what John Arlott told us back in 1970, Bremner's best days were still ahead of him. He lifted Leeds' only FA Cup in 1972, won another Fairs Cup in 1971, and one more League Championship in the 1973-74 season. On two other occasions, in 1971 and '72, Leeds were denied other league championships by one point, taking the race to the final day of the season.

Nor should we forget Leeds and Bremner's one last swansong: their great march to the European Cup Final in 1975. Without Revie, but very much with Bremner at the helm. Only some atrocious refereeing denied Leeds their rightful triumph over Bayern Munich; an injustice that rankles to this day with many Leeds fans.

And should you have ever wanted your key player and captain to pop up in the right place at the right time, Billy Bremner was your man. He scored the decisive goals in three FA Cup semi-finals – 1965 and 1970 against Manchester United; and in 1973 against Wolves. He also scored in the 1965 FA Cup final for Leeds, although they couldn't ultimately deny Liverpool the first FA Cup victory.

There was also the small matter of Scotland's qualification for the 1974 World Cup in West Germany. Bremner captained the team to their first World Cup in 16 years, where the slogan 'Unlucky First Round Losers' would be first painted on their departing coach. One win and two draws meant they would be leaving early, and that Brazil and Yugoslavia would advance to the next phase. But Bremner was the pulsating force behind that team, always urging – never taking a step back.

He was a great captain for Scotland, in an era when the competing claims of those players based in England would be 'de-prioritised', if there were a Scottish player in the Scottish league playing just as well in the same position. That Bremner stood above the likes of McNeill and Greig as a leader, tells us all we need to understand about how great he was at motivating a team.

His international career, sadly, ended after 'a nightclub incident' in Copenhagen, in 1975. A lifetime ban really was not the fitting end for his service to Scotland. By 1976, Billy had also ended his Leeds career, moving to Second Division Hull City.

He did return to manage Leeds in 1985, after starting his new career at Doncaster Rovers. But a replayed play-off final to Division 1 against Charlton Athletic in 1987, was as close as Bremner would come to managerial success at Elland Road. He was sacked in September 1988. Howard Wilkinson succeeded Billy, and was given the money to buy the likes Strachan, McAllister, Speed, Chapman, Lukic and Cantona. Leeds won their last league championship in 1992.

At Leeds, Billy Bremner will always be far more than just a footballer. He is still their benchmark, the key to finding their next generation of great players and leaders. He remains Leeds' greatest-ever player.

For the rest of us, we reminisce and laugh at Dave Mackay calling Billy "…a dirty little bastard". But we also remember that "dirty little bastard", dragging a team of the hardest footballers you had ever seen, by the scruff of the neck, and shouting to them "Follow me!"

Billy Bremner was one small man, but one giant of a human being.

Jack Charlton

The late bloomer; the "foreign" manager

"I like the way you don't trust him."
> Sir Alf Ramsey, on Jack Charlton's playing
> relationship with Bobby Moore

Jack Charlton was abrupt, stood for no-nonsense, a thinker destined for a career in management, once his playing days had finished. Him and his pal at Leeds, Hunter, carried the biggest clout in the 'Dirty Leeds' team. The 'Dirty Big Giraffe' was the awkward sod, who went up for corners, just to stand in front of the goalkeeper; and he had those telescopic legs, to nick the ball away from any advancing attacker. Forever in the shadow of his better-known, prodigiously talented brother Bobby, he was never envious: "He is the greatest player I have ever seen. And he is my brother".

Jack Charlton spent a good few of his early years playing between Division 1 and 2, but always with Leeds, where he would go on to play 629 league games. He was loyal to the team that had first recognised his talent, and he was fortunate enough to enjoy the ride, as their glory years coincided with Charlton's latter playing years.

But he was no passenger. Charlton was the very

foundation of that Leeds team, the leader in defence, one of the antagonists in a referee's ear throughout a match. That one constant, who had endured the struggles of the 50s, and had savoured the victories of the 60s and 70s.

He became so good, in fact, that someone as astute as Sir Alf Ramsey, had spotted a role in his England team for him, next to the best defender in the world, Bobby Moore. Yet another of Ramsey's 'square pegs', Charlton was given his first start for England two days shy of his 30th birthday, in 1965. Thirty-five caps, 21 clean sheets and a World Cup winners' medal later, Charlton (J) had totally vindicated his manager's selection.

But it was the influence of another manager at Leeds in 1961, Don Revie, who transformed the playing abilities and later career of Charlton. Revie's modern methods of coaching – lessons assimilated by English football on a foggy weekday afternoon in November 1953 – allied to a willingness to add the necessary steel on the pitch, allowed him to build a team of genuine greatness, that suddenly asserted itself within English football, during the 1960s. And it saw the blooming of a talent, who up until that time, had never been assessed as anything other than an average player in an inconsistent team.

Initially, Revie didn't rate Charlton. As a player at Leeds, Revie had accused Charlton of messing around as a player, and making it difficult for others at the club with his 'chip on his shoulder'. So, when he became Jack's manager, the writing was being scrawled on the wall in very large letters. In fact, Revie did announce that he was prepared to let him go – but strangely enough, never put him on the transfer list. Two aborted negotiations later at Manchester United (could you imagine!) and Liverpool, Jack decided to stay and impress the new manager at Leeds.

Cue an impressed Revie, letting Jack organise the defence under his preferred zonal-marking system. And then cue promotions, Cup Finals and League Championships. No longer the one-man member of the *Awkward Squad*, the penny dropped, and Jack finally had the playing responsibility he craved.

It took a few near misses, and World Cup glory, before any domestic and European triumphs with Leeds; but steadily, the trophies began to accumulate. One Championship, one FA Cup, two Fairs Cups, and one League Cup – and far too many runners-up medals. And one personal crowning glory, Jack Charlton, the FWA's *Footballer of the Year* in 1967.

But by 1973, an increasingly fragile, 37-year-old, Jack Charlton decided to stop playing football and concentrate on his new career in football management. When second division Middlesbrough offered him a relatively easy path to start that career, he accepted. A season later, Middlesbrough had won the Second Division Championship by 15 points (two points for a win in those days), and in a season when Revie's Leeds had won the First Division title and Shankly's Liverpool had won the FA Cup, it was Jack Charlton who won the *Manager of the Year* award, something unprecedented outside of the First Division.

It looked like the manager's life was a perfect fit for the wise and articulate Jack, but his natural instinct to kick against authority saw him fall out with managerial boards at every club he served. After a promising start with Middlesbrough, he had quit four clubs in eight years, never quite finding his 'home' within a club.

But then, in December 1985, the call came from the Irish FA; and Irish football – and Ireland – would never be the same.

Jack Charlton and Ireland were the perfect fit. Jack already had a house on the west coast, to be closer to his fishing. "I like Ireland. I like the Irish people, I like a pint of Guinness, I like the craic." This relationship was always going to work. And, so, it did.

In the space of 10 years, Ireland rose from continual under-achievers, to a respected footballing nation. An "oh so close" story at the Euros in 1988, and successive qualifications to the latter stages of two World Cups tell most of the story. But sprinkle in a win and a draw against England, a quarter-final appearance in Italia '90, and a win against eventual finalists, Italy, in 1994; and you get some idea of the stratospheric lift that Charlton gave to the team. This was the team, representing a small population 3.5 million in 1990, that had hitherto struggled to assert an identity on the world stage. And this was truly Ireland – and their new manager – breaking new ground: the 'foreign' manager now pointed the way for the 'Home Nations', too.

His approach to coaching and managing a football team was rudimentary: it was better to do simple things well, rather than get involved in complications. It was also about applying pressure to the other team, so that it would be more difficult for that team to play the game of football they wanted to play. This approach didn't suit everyone – including some Irish players – and Charlton's Ireland were soon labelled the *Wimbledon of International Football*, by their jealous detractors. But Jack would always have his belligerent say in response, as he would when his players were labelled 'mercenaries', just because they used their Irish ancestry to play for the Irish national team.

But for the vast, vast majority of Ireland football fans, that did not matter – Ireland had become a respected football nation. And, he, Jack Charlton, had become loved by the people of Ireland. Here was no English politician patronising the Irish people – this was a blunt Geordie, speaking the language of football and life. He did speaking tours to packed audiences around the country, with people leaving the mountains to see him.

Not for nothing, did the people of Ireland bestow upon Jack Charlton, *Freeman of the City of Dublin* and *Honorary Irish citizen*. "He brought us to places we never thought possible," Niall Quinn said. "He changed lives. For his players, he gave us the best days of our lives." Paul McGrath still calls Jack his "guardian angel". The lasting impression he left behind in Ireland is that, maybe, it was the British regime that should be despised, not necessarily all the Brits.

With some of those who had the greatest influence on our game, you can compartmentalise their playing careers and the later managerial careers: their respective achievements within each profession are standalone achievements. But Jack carried all that he was about as a player – the intelligence, the honesty, the disruptive cantankerousness – into his managerial career. The achievements may have varied, but any team he played for, any team he managed, there was always the pulsating energy of Jack Charlton at its core.

He was just a very wonderful football man.

Sir Bobby Charlton

England's Greatest Footballer

"There has never been a more popular footballer. He was as near perfection as man and player as it is possible to be."

Sir Matt Busby

There's a *Two Ronnies* sketch from the 70s, where Ronnie Corbett is in a bar, in an unnamed South American country. He doesn't speak the native language, so shouts loudly in English, in the expectation that the South American barman – a 'bronzed-up' Ronnie Barker – can better understand him. Barker does not understand Corbett. He knows no English dialect. He knows one English name, and one English name only. To every irritated request from Corbett, Barker responds "Bobby Charlton".

Proof, were proof ever needed, that the name of England's greatest-ever footballer was, once, unequivocally etched on the lips of football fans worldwide.

The young, two-footed, Bobby had been spotted at an early age by several clubs. Known to have a family link to Newcastle United's Jackie Milburn – they were second cousins – there may have been an expectation that Bobby would have wanted to join his local team. But even at this

41

early age, he knew that there were other clubs that looked after their young players better than Newcastle. So, as a schoolboy, he decided to join Matt Busby's Manchester United in 1953, turning professional with the club in October 1954.

One European Cup; three league titles; one FA Cup; one *Ballon d'Or*; one FWA award – and one World Cup for England – Charlton quit United, to start a managerial career at Preston North End. The 19-year marriage to United was almost – almost – that marriage made in heaven. However, Bobby Charlton's career in football would forever be marked with one note of great sadness.

As a football player, Bobby Charlton achieved everything he had ever wanted to achieve. A regular winner with his adopted team, a one-time winner – remembered forever – for his country. Feted at one time as the best player in the world, still feted today as England's greatest ever player. But he always carried the scar of Munich – and the burden and the guilt – for the rest of his life.

At the age of 20, in 1958, he physically survived the trauma of the *Munich Air Disaster*, with minor injuries. But he was mentally scarred by the knowledge that eight of his young team-mates didn't complete their return home. As the names of those that hadn't survived the crash were read out to him, Charlton recalled how "my life was being taken away from me, piece by piece".

Bearing witness to such trauma, at such a young age, left an indelible mark. His brother Jack recalled "...a big change in our kid from that day on. He stopped smiling". It was said that introspection now replaced his natural shyness. It was that burden that he carried for the rest of his career, his life, a burden that would have ruined lesser men. That Bobby Charlton could face up to and learn to adapt to his new world, without his team-mates, who had perished at Munich, tells us all we need to know of the man's great mental strength.

And at the heart of Bobby Charlton's new world, was the quest to rebuild Manchester United after Munich. Until that fateful afternoon, United had been the top team in England, manager Matt Busby's revolutionary policy of fielding his 'Babes' bearing fruit over the preceding two seasons. Busby, still recovering from his own injuries, would have to start again. It was his good fortune that he could turn to one of his best players, to maintain the playing standards and traditions of United, as they fought their way back to the summit of English football.

Charlton proved to be the integral component of United's rebuilding process after Munich. He could play anywhere, but Busby played him where he would cause most damage to the opposition. His powerful shooting, athleticism, and great stamina meant that his boss often just needed to point him in the right direction. However, and with the help of United's other two 'greatest players', Best and Law, they both agreed on a permanent switch to a deep-lying forward role. This switch was to prove vital, as Busby's men took their game to the next level, winning two league championships and a European Cup.

All this time, Charlton's England career was purring along. He went to the 1958 World Cup in Sweden, but didn't play a game. By the time he went to Chile in 1962, he had scored 23 goals in 25 games, and managed to score a goal against Argentina at the World Cup. The new man at the helm in 1963, Alf Ramsey, was determined to give England as good a chance as possible to win the next World Cup, hosted on English soil; and he saw Charlton's role as absolutely pivotal in this quest.

And shortly before the 1966 World Cup, Charlton was named *Football Writers' Association Player of the Year* and *European Footballer of the Year* in quick succession – we watched England's greatest ever forward coming to his peak, just when his country most needed him.

England's World Cup campaign stuttered, as they drew 0-0 with Uruguay in their opening match. A game of few chances, and the whispers had started: "Exactly how good are England; is the expectation too much for them on home soil?"

But normality was resumed, and expectations were fulfilled, in the very next match against Mexico. A Charlton right-foot piledriver from 25 yards, set England on their way. They coasted through their group; out-played an Argentinian team that came for a fight in the quarter-final, before landing on a semi-final date with Eusebio and Portugal, at Wembley on a glorious July midweek evening.

That wasn't easy. A nation on a roll, in a football tournament – that kind of momentum is difficult to halt. Host nations had historically done very well in World Cups, reaching, or at least exceeding expectations. But this unheralded Portuguese team had already bundled out Pele and Brazil; and Eusebio had scored four in their 5-3 victory against North Korea in the quarter-final.

No matter in the end. Bobby Charlton turned in his greatest ever England performance, just when his country needed it most. Two goals – one trademark howitzer, one slide-rule pass into the net – were enough to take England into the final, where they would meet old foes West Germany.

We all know the outcome, and we all know that Charlton and Beckenbauer effectively cancelled each other out. But it was this discrete battle – taking the two best attacking players out of the game – that provided the space for others to flourish. Ball's man-of-the-match performance, somehow even overshadowing history-maker Geoff Hurst's hat-trick. A World Cup Final that should have provided the platform for one, maybe two, of the world's greatest attacking midfielders to shine, was remembered for other, equally memorable, reasons.

Bobby Charlton then had to wait two further years to reach the pinnacle of his club career, as he scored two goals and captained United to European Cup glory at Wembley. In the best traditions of this marvellous and emotional footballer, he was reduced to tears, just as he had been at the same venue, two years earlier. But these were the tears he would share with Busby and Bill Foulkes, the other playing survivor from Munich.

There followed a gradual wind-down of his career, as he played his last game for England in the heat of Mexico against West Germany – a game England should never have lost. He managed to avoid the ignominy of United's relegation in 1974, leaving the club at the end of the 1972-73 season, to seize his new opportunity at Preston.

Bobby Charlton went on to become English football's finest ambassador, playing a key role in numerous English World Cup and Olympic Games bids, including the London 2012 Olympic Games campaign. He also he returned to Manchester United as a director in 1984, and developed a close bond with United manager Alex Ferguson; he also assumed further ambassadorial duties as the club developed its own global sporting brand in the 90s.

A total icon of football, his name known and dropped far and wide. That he achieved everything that he did, to become adored as he was, is a testament to his achievements on the pitch, and his warmth and engagement off the pitch.

That all of this was achieved, as this very great man carried his own personal burden, post-Munich, elevates Bobby Charlton to the supreme position within English football.

There was no better man.

Kenny Dalglish

The greatest-ever Scotland-England transfer

"When Kenny shines, the whole team is illuminated"
Bob Paisley

His boss at Liverpool, Bob Paisley, said that. He played in a team with Souness, Hansen, McDermott, Grobbelaar and Lawrenson – and he was the one that lit up THAT team. Kenny Dalglish was truly a very special player.

Kenny Dalglish is a colossus in Liverpool, the living embodiment of all that is great about the football team and the football-mad city. Dalglish brought the team and city glory on the field, and he continued that glory trail as a highly successful manager, when he retired from playing. But he also was the poor guy who bore the weight of a destroyed city upon his shoulders, in the aftermath of Hillsborough – and the people of Liverpool wouldn't have wanted anyone else to carry that weight.

It was Dalglish who ensured that if he couldn't make one of the funerals for the many supporters who perished that day at Hillsborough, somebody else from Liverpool FC would attend; he and his wife Marina once attended four funerals in one day. Later, of course, he was the guy that answered the call from Liverpool in 2011, to come back and sort out a mess of the club's own making, when they sacked Roy Hodgson.

The story of Kenny Dalglish is still never-ending. Even now, he's recently picked up the *BBC's Lifetime Achievement Award*. He's loved and revered everywhere, the adopted son of Liverpool, via Dalmarnock, Glasgow.

But it's the football side where this story lies. The most basic – the best description, you might muster – is that he was the player who made football look so simple, that, watching him, we kidded ourselves we could all do "that".

Dalglish made his way at Celtic, after being rejected at the trial stage for both Liverpool and West Ham, in 1967. A boyhood fan of Rangers, the legend goes that he ran upstairs to remove his Rangers posters from his bedroom wall, when Celtic's assistant manager Sean Fallon came knocking on the door for Kenny's signature.

He then inched his way into the first team by the 1971-72 season, along with his fellow cohort from the *Quality Street Gang*, the group of young players nursed along to replace the Lisbon Lions of '67. Macari, Hay, McGrain, Connolly, Dalglish – they made that first team even better. But a series of poor boardroom decisions meant that by 1975, only Dalglish and McGrain remained at the club. However, the trophies were stacking up aplenty, and a run to the 1974 European Cup semi-final had hinted at what was potentially around the corner. But a call from Liverpool in 1977 was to change everything for both Kenny Dalglish and for Liverpool.

For every football fan who wished Liverpool legend Kevin Keegan well on his transfer from Liverpool to SV

Hamburg in 1977, there stood at least one to even up the score. The latter group of fans – cheered on by the tabloids – labelled Keegan a mercenary for wanting to increase his wages from £12,500 a year to £250,000 a year. They may have had a fair point, if Keegan hadn't have returned back to Division 1 in 1980, with an armful of trophies, including two *Ballon d'Ors*.

But the most magnificent consolation for this group of fans was found in Keegan's replacement, Kenny Dalglish. Dalglish had joined in the summer, for a British transfer fee record of £440,000, and 31 goals later, including the winner against FC Bruges at Wembley in the European Cup Final, these fans were now referring to their recently departed idol as "Kevin Who?"

Dalglish made a great start to his Liverpool career, scoring in his first four games, and carrying on that goal-scoring form for the rest of that 1977-78 season. We all knew who he was in England; we'd seen all the Saturday lunchtime clips on *Football Focus* and we'd even caught a few glimpses of him at the last World Cup in Germany. If Celtic were doing well in Europe, we might see a bit more of him, and, obviously, there was the England v Scotland live match in the Home Internationals.

But that's it, that's all we saw. At that time, what was to tell us in England that Kenny Dalglish wouldn't be just another Scot coming south of the border, having been signed for a big fee, and not quite coping with the extra demands of Division 1 in England? Granted, there had been a few Scots over the years who had coped. But for every Mackay, Crerand, Yeats and Macari, there were a few more Ures, Marinellos, Baxters and Hays. What we ended up with Kenny Dalglish is a player who became the very best cross-border transfer ever; and way beyond even that, we had a player who has claims to be Britain's greatest-ever footballer.

Over the period 1977-83, peak Dalglish, we watched a player develop his huge skillset as his own game matured, simply because he was surrounded by better players. As always, his modesty would credit his successes to those others around him. And he attributes his development at Liverpool to one man: "I owe Bob more than I owe anybody else in the game". It was the Paisley way to have his team play as a collective force, to never stop running, to keep possession and to create scoring opportunities. And Dalglish found it easy to be on the receiving end of all that work that went into setting up no end of those 'scoring opportunities'.

But it was Kenny Dalglish, the maestro, who didn't just finish it all off. That just sounds too easy. It looked easy, but that was because you were watching Kenny Dalglish do it. This was the guy who ran into a space that no one noticed was free, that no one else knew would be the exact spot where the ball would land.

It was that vision, that awareness, that ability to stand still for a split-second longer than anybody else, that separated him for the rest. That extra split-second timing meant that he would finish clinically with either foot; or, increasingly from 1981 onwards, lay on the defence-splitting pass for strike partner Ian Rush to run onto and score. And woe betide any defender who did manage to get near Dalglish when he took control of the ball. A swift turn of the hips would often leave that defender on the deck – if Kenny Dalglish bumped you, you stayed bumped.

Six Championships; three European Cups; one FA Cup; four League Cups later, he'd wrapped up his playing career at Liverpool FC. Paisley had built Liverpool's greatest team, and Kenny Dalglish had become Liverpool's greatest ever player. Internationally, we should never forget, too, that he played at three World Cups, and is Scotland's leading goalscorer, alongside Denis Law.

He did, Kenny Dalglish lit up everything around him. He was so good that he shone as the beacon in the greatest team, arguably, that English football has ever produced.

You don't need to dwell on his many managerial achievements, his role as Liverpool FC's greatest-ever ambassador. He was the football player who gave so much joy to so many people, Liverpool fan or not.

The guy just shone.

Derek Dougan

The Showman

"The complete enigma. Electrification and exasperation.
Poise and petulance – a mass of contradictions"
The *Daily Mirror*'s sportswriter, Frank McGhee

Portsmouth; Blackburn Rovers; Aston Villa; Peterborough United; Leicester City – all the teams Derek Dougan played for between 1957-67. Not bad going in 10 years. But throw in a transfer request on the eve of the FA Cup Final, whilst playing at Blackburn, and the numerous run-ins with the clubs he played for, and you get a clearer picture of the turmoil that tended to surround *The Doog*.

But in 1967, he did, finally, find the true love of his football life at Wolverhampton Wanderers, the club where he settled until his retirement from football in 1975.

In many ways, Dougan was made for this era; he was its perfect participant. His flamboyant presence demanded a larger audience than a mere football stadium and a few journalists, to draft the story of that afternoon's events. If he hadn't scored a goal, there would have been something else to record: a protracted discussion with a referee/opposing player; a dispute with just about everybody else on the pitch. So, when football did arrive on our screens in the mid-60s, television became that vehicle that both elevated Dougan's persona and sometimes, unfortunately, diminished him as a person.

Derek Dougan made his way into English football, via Distillery in his native Belfast. He helped Distillery to win the Irish Cup in 1956, before a £4,000 move to English First Division side Portsmouth in August 1957. He was sold on to Blackburn Rovers in March 1959 for a fee of £15,000. And whilst at Portsmouth, he appeared at the 1958 World Cup, playing one game for Northern Ireland against Czechoslovakia.

But it was that transfer request on the eve of the 1960 FA Cup Final, that really brought Derek Dougan to the attention of the wider football world. There are disputed versions as to why he did this. One, is that he, along with his other teammates, wanted to present a united front to the management of Blackburn Rovers, to extract agreed bonuses that were promised for reaching the final, but hadn't been forthcoming. Except, at the last minute, his teammates didn't follow through with their transfer requests, and left Dougan high and dry.

And there's the other version, which paints Dougan in a very poor light, indeed. That there were doubts about a pulled hamstring and his fitness for the final, and that he put in a transfer request as a threat because he didn't want to miss the final. The tragedy for Blackburn is that Dave Whelan broke a leg in that final, as they lost 3-0 to Wolves, with nine and a half players. Dougan was never forgiven, by a large section of the Rovers' fans.

There then followed two-year spells at each of Aston Villa, Peterborough United – he dropped to the Third Division, just to escape Villa – and Leicester City. Never settled, never happy, a player who was now gaining a reputation of not taking the game seriously, always instigating a fall out with managers.

But it was the move to Second Division Wolves in 1967, that provided the platform for Dougan to finally shine on a consistent basis, and to become the player he had always promised to be. His skillset was seen by a larger audience, as his aggression, bravery and sheer presence, unsettled the best defences. The Doog was soon idolised at Wolves. In 11 appearances, Dougan scored nine goals, after his signing, which proved the vital difference to Wolves achieving promotion from the Second Division. He soon became the fans' favourite, a figure the faithful at Molineux had yearned for, since the end of the glory days in 1960.

Soon he had built up a scoring relationship with winger Dave Wagstaff and inside-forward Peter Knowles, which enabled Wolves to settle comfortably in the First Division. Never quite consistent enough to run the big boys close, but talented enough to turn them over occasionally.

And as a reminder that controversy often walked hand-in-hand with Dougan, he received a post-war record eight-match ban in 1969, for verbally abusing a linesman against Everton, at Molineux. The fans started a mini-riot in the stands as he was sent off, and 84 fans were injured. All in a day's work for Derek Dougan.

His greatest days were actually in the last years of his playing career. He struck up a formidable strike partnership with John Richards, as Wolves qualified for and reached the UEFA Cup Final in 1972, and Wolves were consistent top half of the table finishers at this time. They also came so close to beating Leeds in the 1973 FA Cup semi-final at Maine Road; but it was the 1974 League Cup Final, beating the favourites Man City – Bell, Marsh, Lee, Law and all – 2-1, that proved to be Dougan and Wolves crowning glory. Derek Dougan retired from professional football the following season.

It was during the 70s, that Dougan cultivated a persona off the field, too. Firstly, as a panellist on ITV's coverage of the World Cups in Mexico and West Germany; and secondly, as the Chair of the Professional Footballer's Association (PFA). There was also the role he played in putting an "All-Ireland Team" together, to play Brazil in 1973. Sadly for Dougan, it was a move, he claimed, that would spell the end of his playing career with Northern Ireland.

Dougan and television were a great match. He was stylish, colourful, and, more than anything else, he was articulate. He and Paddy Crerand were a great bickering match, pitched against the slightly boozed charm of Malcolm Allison, during ITV's Mexico '70 programme. Four years later, the three of them appeared together again, on the panel that covered the World Cup in West Germany.

The game against Brazil was never sanctioned by the respective FAs in Ireland and Northern Ireland, so 'Ireland' played as a 'Shamrock Rovers XI'. The game was played at the height of *The Troubles*, and it was Dougan and Johnny Giles who were the protagonists in persuading their team-mates that the game would act as a perfect goodwill gesture.

But it's Dougan's great work as Chair of the PFA, where his greatest off-field legacy lies. Even though the maximum wage had been abolished in the early 60s, clubs, in the 70s, still possessed the power to withhold an out-of-contract player's registration. This meant that the club still 'owned' that player, and didn't have to release them, even if the player wanted to play elsewhere.

His successor as PFA Chair, Gordon Taylor, summed it up "Derek led as chairman, and this brought in the player's right to move in 1978, which was actually the forerunner of Bosman".

There was a flamboyance about Derek Dougan, that is rarely seen on a football pitch. Undoubtedly, there was a steely inner-confidence to underpin the showmanship, and no shortage of ego announcing to the world that he was right. But he also cared about others. He was a great advocate for footballers' rights; and it was his bravery that sought to unite football in Ireland, on a one-off occasion, during its most troubled times.

TV and football provided the perfect stage for this utterly imperfect man.

Trevor Francis

From teenage sensation, to revered veteran

> *"Trevor Francis has died at the age of 69...On behalf of the family, this has come as a huge shock to everybody. He was a legendary footballer, but he was also an extremely nice person"*
>
> Trevor Francis' family

Trevor Francis was a proper teenage sensation at Birmingham City, and scored 15 goals in his first season from 22 games, as a 16-year-old. So, why did it take him 280 appearances and 118 goals for Birmingham City, before anyone noticed his talents?

The truth probably lies within the quotation above. Trevor Francis did, in fact, have six transfer requests rejected by Birmingham. But he wouldn't kick up a fuss, call a one-man strike, or refuse to play in the reserves, because "It wouldn't have been possible for me to do that, because of my character."

He was just an extremely nice person.

Trevor Francis was also the one where a journalist first used the phrase "with a drop of a shoulder, he was away". Or he should have been. Because that's what he did. He was so quick, so skilful, he just sped away from defenders. He used that wonderful balance and guile to have those defenders turning around, arse on the floor, before they could even think of a tackle. And we loved him doing that – especially when he was a kid, and we were about his age.

He did finally get his move away in March 1979, to Brian Clough and Nottingham Forest. Yes, the first British million-pound player. But any pressure attached to that barely-believable price-tag (double the previous British transfer record) was relieved in Munich's Olympic stadium three months later, when a Francis diving header settled the small matter of a European Cup Final, against Malmo. Trevor Francis had finally arrived on a stage, befitting his talents.

He had also accumulated a few England caps, by the time he had transferred to Forest. But there was competition all around for the favoured spot of support role to Kevin Keegan. Who would work best with our two-time 'European Footballer of the Year'? Keegan's needs would rightly come first, but it wasn't just a case of sticking the next best striker alongside him up front – the 'partnership' had to work. Ron Greenwood had variously tried Latchford; Woodcock; Johnson; and Francis over the previous year. England were still winning games, but they hadn't settled on the partnership to take them to the next level.

Then, suddenly, it seemed to click. England went to Barcelona, and handed out a football lesson to Spain, in a warm-up friendly, ahead of the 1980 European Championships. Francis played his best game for England, and scored a goal; and Keegan dropped his hand grenades everywhere, as England ran out easy 2-0 winners. It should have been a few more.

Francis then scored two goals against Dynamo Berlin in the second leg of the quarter-final, and the opening goal against Ajax in the first leg of the semi-final, to get Forest to their second consecutive European Cup final. The boy of 25 was hitting his peak, and it was no exaggeration to suggest that, with Francis on board, England would have two winners in Europe before the season's end.

And then, bang. A ruptured Achilles tendon picked up in a league match against Crystal Palace, spelt the end of Trevor Francis' season. As Clough explained. "At the time of his injury, the lad was going like a bomb".

In a fashion, that only Clough could manage, he stuck an 18-year-old Gary Mills up front in Francis' place for the final against Kevin Keegan's Hamburg, whilst not even filling the allocated five spaces on the substitutes bench. Inevitably, Forest beat Hamburg 1-0 in the European Cup Final, in Madrid. All without his million-pound striker, who Clough had banned from travelling with the party, whilst he continued his recovery on crutches.

England, sadly, did not fare as well. The loss of Francis over three group games inevitably weakened their cause, as they returned home early with a perfect, but costly, 1-1-1 record. Of even greater sadness, Trevor Francis had played the best football of his career, by the age of 25.

He stayed a further 18 months at Forest, not returning to the team until September 1980. Trevor Francis was never the same player after that injury. That 'zip' had left his game; he'd lost that vital half-yard he had on every defender. He, inevitably, suffered further niggly injuries, forcing Clough's hand in September 1981 to accept Man City's offer of £1.2m, to take Francis away from the City Ground.

He did actually play well enough at Man City, to earn a recall to the England set-up. The goals weren't flowing at the old rate, but Francis was still a potent force in Division 1, partially-knackered Achilles, or otherwise. So much so, that he was part of the squad that travelled to Spain for the 1982 World Cup. England faltered, as too much time and energy was expended on the injuries to Keegan and Brooking; but Francis at least had the consolation of scoring twice in the group games.

Newly-promoted Sampdoria then signed Francis, after the World Cup. Trevor and his wife, Helen, loved it there, and spent five years in Italy in total; including a year at Atalanta. Sampdoria won their first-ever Coppa Italia in 1985, with Francis top scoring with nine goals in that season's competition. And even though he remained, to some extent, out of sight, new England manager Bobby Robson consistently picked Francis in his squads.

There then followed a return to Britain, to play for former Sampdoria team-mate Graeme Souness' Rangers, before moving south to end his career, playing first for QPR, and then Sheffield Wednesday. It was during his spell as Wednesday's player-manager, that Trevor Francis finally retired from playing football, a few days shy of his 40th birthday in 1994. The teenage sensation at 16 had finally hung his boots up, 24 years later.

It's the longevity of Trevor Francis' career that is the standout. You would never have thought that a 16-year-old, back in 1970, would last so long in the game. A player as talented and as young as that, would rightly have expected to burn out 10-15 years later, or have achieved all he wanted from the game, within that same timeframe. Instead, he just kept ploughing on, coming back for more.

His England career – 52 games, 12 goals – is no great shakes. But the Achilles injury from 1980, ensured that he was fighting a losing battle to maintain those standards that had taken him to the pinnacle of the game. He proved his worth in four different countries, too, when we include his two very successful half-season stints, playing for Detroit Express in the NASL.

We only had a glimpse of peak-Trevor Francis, and you wonder if this might have been his motivation to prolong his career for as long as he did. He knew that peak had been cruelly taken away from him by injury. Did he then decide that he wanted to get the very most out of his career, in the only remaining way he could?

We were all cruelly denied a proper look of Trevor Francis at his peak. But we were, instead, treated to a full view of this "extremely nice person" over a 24-year playing career.

Jimmy Greaves

Redefining the art of goalscoring

"He wasn't a thumper of the ball, he was a placer"
Terry Paine, ex-England team-mate

There's a very small queue that makes up the 'Greatest Ever English Striker'. You'd have to include the likes of Dean, Lofthouse, Milburn from the baggy-shorts era; and you would, undoubtedly, include the likes of Shearer, Rooney and Kane from the more modern era. But in terms of scoring a goal – who you are trusting your life to score a goal for you – the order goes something like this:

Jimmy Greaves-Daylight-The rest.

Jimmy Greaves still holds all the records, 53 years after he retired from professional football at the highest level. Jimmy scored 357 top-flight goals between 1957-71; he was top scorer in Division One a record six times; he scored a club record 37 league goals for Spurs in the 1962/63 season; and also found the time to score 44 goals in 57 England games. None of those England goals were penalties, by the way. In fact, he only scored 25 penalties in his entire career.

It was just the way he did it. He said it himself "I just picked a spot." Said like scoring a goal – that many goals – was the easiest thing in the world. And it was. For

Jimmy Greaves. He knew where to move to, how to take the ball, and he knew that his pace would take him away from any defender. Once he had sight of goal, he knew that his ice-cold brain would calibrate exactly where to place the ball – "just pick a spot" – and he would adjust his body to the shooting position within a millisecond. Absolute deadeye.

Jimmy Greaves started his career at Chelsea, aged 17, scoring 132 goals in 169 appearances for the Blues, before a transfer to AC Milan in 1960. He went to Milan for the money, shortly before the Football League relented and abolished the maximum wage. Fourteen games and 9 goals later, Jimmy found himself back in England with Spurs, and not a lira to show for his efforts in Italy, as he had broken the terms of his contract by returning to England.

He joined Spurs' double-winning squad, for the famous £99,999 fee in December 1961. He went on to score 266 goals in 379 appearances. He also scored the goals when it mattered, in the FA Cup Final in 1962, and twice in the Cup Winners' Cup Final against Atletico Madrid as Spurs became the first British team to triumph in Europe in 1963. Jimmy was also part of the team that lifted the FA Cup again in 1967.

His Spurs career came to an end in 1970, when he was used as the 'makeweight' in a swap deal that took Martin Peters to Spurs from West Ham. Some comedown for England's greatest ever goal scorer, but, in truth, Jimmy's Spurs career had been on the wane for some time, scoring only eight league goals in his final 29 matches. Jimmy Greaves finished his glorious Tottenham Hotspur career in the reserves.

Jimmy finished his playing career, at the highest level, in 1971 with West Ham, declining Brian Clough's offer of a contract at Derby. The greatest goal-scorer the English game had ever known, almost slid out of the game unnoticed.

Jimmy Greaves' England career is probably best remembered for the game he didn't play. There is the small matter of Jimmy retiring his England career as their record goal-scorer, with 44 goals in 57 games; but this is often overshadowed by Jimmy's non-appearance in the biggest game in the history of English football, the 1966 World Cup Final at Wembley. And the issue is worth exploring, particularly how it shows Jimmy in a very favourable light, years after the event.

Admittedly, it is the professional relationship that Jimmy had with Alf Ramsey, which serves up the slightly sour taste to Jimmy's overall career. However, from 1963 until the build-up to the World Cup in '66, Ramsey always picked Jimmy. He even played Jimmy in the three group games at the World Cup, before a French defender raked his studs down Jimmy's shin, forcing him to miss the next match, the quarter-final against Argentina. But you could never criticise Ramsey for neglecting Greaves, for not giving him every chance to play for England.

However, something always lingered between the pair. Ramsey was loathe to accommodate the one player who showed an occasional lack of effort, whilst nine other outfield players ran like mad for 90 minutes. He would have preferred not to have accommodated the one player who was overly frivolous, who made everything look ridiculously easy, not giving 100% because he didn't have to. And

Ramsey grew tired of Greaves' passive stubbornness – "I'll do it my way". But Ramsey also knew full well that he would accommodate Greaves, because he had to.

But, in the background, Ramsey was noting the progress of a striker at West Ham, who would run all day for his team, score plenty of goals, and take some of the strain off Greaves' strike-partner, Roger Hunt of Liverpool.

Events did actually conspire against Jimmy, and to Ramsey's favour anyway. In November 1965, Jimmy suffered a bout of Hepatitis B, keeping him out of the game for three months. This was no minor illness, and Jimmy's consultant had warned him that he would never be the same player again, that he would lose a bit of his sharpness. Greaves admits that this is exactly what did happen – for the rest of his career, he wasn't as fast, his reactions were slower. See how his goal scoring ratio tails off slightly in his Spurs career, post-1966.

So, when Jimmy had those 12 stitches in his shin after the France match, Ramsey was presented with the perfect opportunity to introduce Geoff Hurst into the England team. Hurst had only played for England five times before the game against Argentina, but history now records that Hurst scored the winner in that game; laid a goal on a plate for Bobby Charlton in the semi-final against Portugal; and banged in the perfect hat-trick in the final against West Germany. Ramsey vindicated; a nation rejoices – the perfect script.

Except, poor Jimmy is left as 'the loneliest man in the stadium', at the end of the game.

In truth, Jimmy's lack of form left him vulnerable to being dropped anyway. He hadn't scored a goal in England's three group matches (his strike partner, Hunt, had scored three in three matches), and his lack of sharpness had been noted. However, he would have been fit for the final, 10 days after having those stitches. But Ramsey couldn't take that chance, not in the days where substitutions were not allowed. And, anyway, Geoff Hurst had seized his opportunity with both feet.

Luckily, nearly 60 years later, we're not having that conversation where Greaves had unforgivably conned Ramsey into playing him in the final and England had lost.

It's sad that we still debate the one game, that Jimmy didn't play. He deserves to be remembered and celebrated for much more than that. But, to Jimmy Greaves' eternal credit, he bore absolutely no ill-feeling towards Ramsey and Hurst; in fact, he became closer to both of them, after they had all retired.

Ramsey had a horrible decision to make – someone would wear a scar for the rest of their lives because of it. Jimmy was devastated at the time – who wouldn't have been? But Ramsey had also dropped Ball, Connelly, Paine and Callaghan during the tournament, as he sought to get that absolutely perfect blend on the pitch. His single-minded vision won England its only ever World Cup. Celebrate that.

But also celebrate Jimmy knowing, eventually, that Alf had made the correct decision, despite his own great disappointment.

Celebrate Jimmy Greaves the great man, who bore no grudge.

Celebrate Jimmy Greaves, that one player who made scoring a goal look like the easiest thing in the world to do.

Jimmy Hill

The noisy revolutionary

"It's all very well having good ideas, but most of his ideas became part of football's fabric"

England great, Gary Lineker

If you were lucky enough to have watched the game of football in the 60s and 70s, you would have done well to keep up with everything that was going on. The game was changing at such a pace, that it became unrecognisable from the same game fans had watched in the ten years that had preceded it.

For the first time, we had players earning £100 a week, and, for the first time, we saw these players on our new TV screens, in our actual homes. To add a further layer of glitz and the glamour to all this, by the end of the 70s, nearly every household in the country watched these well-paid players on a colour TV.

And there's one constant thread – one player, Trade Union rep, manager, pundit, TV Head of Sport, "noisy revolutionary" – running through all of this flux.

Jimmy Hill played professional football for Brentford and Fulham. He played nearly 400 games and spent most of his career in the second and third divisions, once setting a

Fulham club record, by scoring five goals for Fulham against Doncaster Rovers in 1958. He was also part of the team that gained promotion to the First Division in 1959. His football playing career wasn't much to write home about.

However, in 1957, Jimmy Hill became *Chair of the Professional Footballers' Association* (PFA). We were now playing a quite different ball game.

Under Hill's leadership, the PFA suddenly became more vocal. For almost the entirety of its existence, the Football League had imposed a 'maximum wage' that footballers could be paid. By 1961, the most any footballer could earn in the English football league was £20 per week. In the 1901-02 season, the maximum wage had stood at £4 per week.

The imposition of this maximum wage meant that there existed very little movement of players between clubs. Why would a player move to the other end of the country just to be paid exactly what he'd been paid at his previous club? And this, in turn, led to a far greater equality between teams; all the teams paid the same wage; therefore, teams were not forced to sell, and could nurture their home-grown talent.

In the years 1946-1960, there were eight separate winners of the football league and 12 different winners of the FA Cup. This is exactly how football looked to the fans from this era, with an expectation that this would always be the case.

But it was the abolition of the maximum wage – brought about by the threat of strike action by the players in 1961 – which proved to be the significant moment in English football. It preceded the seismic change, which helped to develop the game over the course of the most important era in football, into becoming the glamourous game that it is today.

And it is no flight of fancy to suggest that it is Jimmy Hill, who has subsequently emerged as the most important figure in that development of English football, over the past 60 years.

His job done as a PFA Chair, Jimmy Hill retired as a player in November 1961 to become the manager of Third Division Coventry City. With his now familiar agitating zeal, his time spent at the club until 1967, marked 'The Sky Blue Revolution'. Promoted all the way to Division One by 1967, he introduced the first colour matchday match programme to English football; chartered trains to away games; and even had the first electronic scoreboard installed at Highfield Road.

But there was more to come, inevitably, as Jimmy Hill now moved into broadcasting. Firstly, into the role of London Weekend Television's Head of Sport; and then to co-host The Big Match. the London version of the ITV network's Sunday lunchtime football highlights package. And if you were lucky enough, and your TV transmitter/ receiver thing picked up LWT's programmes, you could even watch *The Big Match* in the far-flung villages of the Home Counties.

He and co-host Brian Moore were a very likeable twosome, but they were never afraid to confront the poor behaviours that they saw as creeping into the game. Showing dissent to referees, poor tackling, feigning injuries, were all given the same treatment from Hill and Moore – they took their love of football very seriously. They were also lucky enough to interview players from the previous day's matches in the LWT studios, often showing our heroes away from a football field for the first time, and unashamedly wearing a fashionable jumper of the time.

And it was The Big Match, and ITV's overall excellent coverage of football, that served as a precursor to *Mexico '70*, that totally revolutionary ITV football broadcast, covering the 1970 World Cup. You'd either watch the live match, scrutinised by the panel; or you'd watch highlights of the matches the BBC had shown live, scrutinised by the panel. During the 1970 World Cup, you could even watch the football, whilst eating your breakfast!

And what a panel ITV – Jimmy Hill and executive producer John Bromley, in particular – served up: Dougan, Crerand, McNab and Allison. All expertly marshalled by Hill and Moore. The stubborn and argumentative pairing of Dougan and Crerand, set against the cool-as you-like 'Big Mal', fuelled by a supply of champagne and cigars. ITV were forced to issue the junior partner McNab with a bell, just so that he could get a word in edgeways. Throw in first time-ever slow-motion replays; a crackling satellite transmission and a World Cup shown in colour for the first time, and we were treated to a visual and audio spectacle, the like of which we had never witnessed before. No wonder that ITV – for the first and only time – beat the Beeb in the World Cup ratings war.

It was football, the greatest sport on earth, which was now broadcasting 'The Greatest Show on Earth'. Whether you loved football or you loathed it, you were now going to watch it. That football and that panel were irresistible.

Jimmy Hill then switched sides to the BBC in 1973, maintaining a weekly presence on our TV screens, by hosting *Match of the Day*, and often acting as a pundit. And it was at this time, more as a pundit, that he displayed a hint of irascibility and more of his own need to be controversial. But, also, simultaneously, he still looked for improvements to the game that he loved, becoming a great advocate for 'Three points for a win', to make the game more attractive.

Undoubtedly, he gradually moved beyond the 'marmite' character he had always been, to more of a universal character of scorn and derision. Scottish fans particularly disliked him. Describing David Narey's outstanding strike from the edge of the area to take the lead against Brazil at the 1982 World Cup as "a toe-poke", did not sit well with disgruntled Scottish fans, who had to watch their team depart a World Cup on goal difference for the third consecutive time. It didn't sit too well with some of us elsewhere, too, suspecting Hill's comments were nothing other than a xenophobic jibe at our friends north of the border.

He continued his direct association within football, by taking up directorships at Fulham and Charlton. And he breathed new life into his broadcasting career, joining Sky in 1999, to host the always-absorbing *Jimmy Hill's Sunday Supplement*. He was good at that, chairing a discussion where he let the journalists do the talking – he assumed a far more neutral stance in his later days, and we learned to love him again.

Jimmy Hill should always be remembered for his immense contribution to football. He immersed himself in the game, because he loved the game. He did nothing but good for the game, his own passion always shining through. Whether as a Chair of the PFA, an innovative manager and football man, or just a great broadcaster, we will remember him well.

Jimmy Hill participated in football's greatest era, and, still, he remains that era's greatest participant.

Sir Geoff Hurst

The first of the modern-day forwards

"You're a horrible defender. When the ball goes behind, you don't know where you are"

> Ron Greenwood, just before he converted
> Geoff Hurst to an attacker

There was one week in Geoff Hurst's career – 23-30 July 1966 – that not only transformed his life, but also the lives of 21 other players and one particular member of the England football team managerial staff. For many supporters of the England football team, that week, whilst not transforming their lives, 'mattered' to them for the rest of their lives. And Geoff Hurst is still, 58 years later, very much a point of reference, our source of great comfort, every time an England football team doesn't win a tournament.

The story of Geoff Hurst's involvement in England's World Cup victory in 1966, should be viewed as a whole. A mere squad member, in the days before substitutes, he didn't anticipate a starting role, let alone a starring role. He had only made his debut against West Germany in the February. He was content, like teammate Martin Peters, to cheer from the sidelines, but always ready to step up, should Sir Alf Ramsey call for him.

However, a shin injury to out-of-form Jimmy Greaves meant that Sir Alf did, indeed, have to turn to his West Ham striker – he of the great hold up play, tireless running, a thunderbolt in each foot – to fill the void in the quarter final tie against Argentina. This, the new, modern-day forward, who wouldn't just hang around a goal, waiting for chances to be fed to him.

Cue the start of one monumental week in English football.

Ramsey's view was that strike partner Roger Hunt needed someone next to him, who would do the same amount of running as him, harass defenders in the same way, and create the same chances for themselves and England's midfield. One week, four goals and one and a half assists later, Geoff Hurst would be a World Cup winner. And it is not too fanciful to suggest, that it was Geoff Hurst who made the vital difference between England winning and losing the 1966 World Cup tournament.

It's easy to make a case that Geoff Hurst's contribution to England's World Cup win has been underplayed over the years. And it's easy to see why: he played in a team that was full of world-class players, all slightly above Hurst's level. The narrative runs something like "He was lucky to get a look in, and it was the contribution of the other, better, players, that really won the World Cup for England".

There also exists, still, an undercurrent of resentment, that Hurst took the place of a fully fit Jimmy Greaves for the final. But nor is it an exaggeration, to suggest that we just weren't used to this style of play from forwards on a football pitch. We were far more used to strikers lurking near the opposing goal, just waiting for a chance to score. We were far less used to watching strikers actually creating chances for themselves and other team-mates.

However, Geoff Hurst had to play as Greaves' replacement against Argentina in the quarter-final. He went on to score the only goal of the game, to beat a talented and stubborn team, who themselves had stopped West Germany from scoring in the group stages. A goal created on the training ground at West Ham, Hurst flicking on a near-post header, from a whipped-in Martin Peters cross.

In the semi-final, his unselfish awareness had laid a pass on a plate for Bobby Charlton to score England's crucial second goal against Portugal. He now simply had to play in the final. Greaves hadn't scored in any of the three group games, and couldn't be risked, as there wasn't a substitute allowed to replace him, should his injury recur.

What happened next is something that has never been repeated. England won the World Cup; and a player scored a hat-trick for the winning team. At that stage, you may well have thought, that's it for the guy who scored the goals – and is even involved in the goal he didn't score. Made for life, feted forever. He will never reach those heights again, that's one week that will never be repeated in his career. But we shall recognise this massive contribution immediately – Geoff Hurst will win every award going, that year.

But no. Bobby Moore won the *BBC Sports Personality of the Year* in 1966. Bobby Charlton won the *Ballon d'Or*, with Geoff Hurst in 14th place, securing two votes. Ahead of him in the voting were Charlton, Moore, Ball and Banks.

Hurst ranked fifth in importance to the England World Cup winning effort. The bloke who made the difference in a keenly and evenly contested final; the bloke who scored the perfect hat-trick, to secure England's World Cup win was considered to be England's fifth most important player? You might assume that Alan Ball won his place above Hurst, because of his 'Man of the Match' contribution in the final, "running himself daft"? But 'Man of the Match', above Hurst?

The easiest comparison to this injustice is Paolo Rossi, Italy's stylish striker and hero of Italy's 1982 World Cup victory. Six goals in three games secured the win, including a hat-trick against Brazil (effectively, in a quarter-final). All this, after Rossi had served a two-year ban for his part in a football betting scandal (Sir Geoff Hurst would never have been involved in anything like that, by the way!). World Cup winner and *Ballon d'Or* winner that year, both he and Hurst finished with very similar international records.

But it's probably best that it transpired that way. A humble, uncomplicated man, Hurst realised the full worth of what he had done. He was happy to go home to his family after the World Cup Final, and mow the lawn the next day. Perfectly content at West Ham, he didn't chase a big money move elsewhere.

West Ham had given him everything he wanted in football, and he'd even scored a goal in the 1964 FA Cup Final, to help his team beat Preston North End. So, when Ron Greenwood rejected Manchester United's British record bid of £200k to take Geoff to Old Trafford in 1967, he was happy to stay at Upton Park. Not for Geoff Hurst the threat of a strike, or demanding an instant pay rise.

Geoff Hurst knew himself what he had done; it was for others to argue his greater worth. He doesn't regret anything from his playing career, nor does he resent today's players' vast earnings. If he had been showered with more awards, more praise, maybe this would have upset the delicate balancing act of preserving a bit of himself and his young family. If he had courted greater publicity, that surely would only have come back to impact his family.

Geoff Hurst, alongside Martin Peters, even spent the best part of 20 years in the insurance industry, after their playing careers had finished. They still had to provide for their families, and neither were above cold-calling a few people on behalf of *Abbey Life*. That was the life of an ex-footballer in the 80s; even the ones who had won their country a World Cup.

From everything you see and know of him now, on documentary, or in books, his own tour, Geoff Hurst maintains that unreal humility. England's one surviving player from that incredible summer's day in 1966 – the most important part of the jigsaw on that day, the 'difference'. He should be venerated forever; he is our national treasure.

He is our greatest living Englishman, whether he wants to be, or not.

Kevin Keegan

English football's greatest export

"I was just as sure of Keegan as I was of Denis Law, and I never had cause to think again about Denis. These two players are so much alike in many ways."
Bill Shankly, on his new signing at Liverpool

It is easy to argue that Kevin Keegan never quite gets the recognition he deserves.

There are a few reasons for this. Firstly, he had to work so hard to get his break, and then to become the player that he became – his talent never seemed to be "God-given". Secondly, his recognition as Europe's best player, twice, occurred in a relatively weak era, post-Beckenbauer and Cruyff. And, thirdly, his successor at Liverpool has a claim to be an even better player than King Kev.

He did the hard yards, no one can argue with that, starting at Division 4 team Scunthorpe. A season and a bit after his 'break' – a transfer to Liverpool – he played for England, a testament to where the application of hard work and talent can lead to.

He stayed at Scunthorpe for three seasons, ending with a pretty meagre return of 18 goals in 124 games. But it was his ability to "drop a few hand grenades" that appealed to his next boss, Bill Shankly. The energy levels, the willingness to run directly at and through defenders with his staccato dribbling; his genuine pace over 10 yards; that colossal work ethic – this all made Keegan an irresistible talent.

A five-season stay at Liverpool followed, where he proved himself as the best player in the football league. He made it his own mission to grab that chance, a chance he would easily have thought would pass him by, playing for a team that didn't even challenge for promotion from Division 4. His game improved, to the extent that he and his new strike-partner, John Toshack, took on the best defences in Division 1, and, generally, had the better of them. A League Championship and UEFA Cup were just rewards for their 1972-73 campaign, but it was a three-month period the following year, when the country became increasingly aware of this exciting young talent.

And it is no exaggeration to suggest that Kevin Keegan stole the headlines in many of the newspapers, front and back, for a lengthy period between May and August 1974.

It all started with the Cup Final, and Liverpool's 90-minute dissection of Joe Harvey's humble Newcastle team, led upfront by an immodest braggart. The wayward predictions of 'Supermouth' Malcolm Macdonald were soon forgotten, as Wembley, and the nation, were treated to an almost solo performance from Kevin Keegan. He totally ran the show that afternoon, scoring two goals, as Liverpool won 3-0. He was at his bustling, busy best, demanding the ball, orchestrating the play. He fitted that Liverpool team so well that day, and you understood exactly why Shankly loved him so much.

The very next month, we saw Kevin almost beaten to a

pulp, by over-officious Yugoslav police at Belgrade Airport! It was all a case of very-badly mistaken identity, with the England players arriving in Belgrade an hour early, and not wearing their more formal 'England' attire. The police were also alerted to some mild misbehaviour from the touring party. FA officials did manage to persuade the police to release Keegan, but not before he had been hauled into a private room for his very own private beating.

Two days later, an unbelievably focussed Keegan grabbed a 75th minute equaliser in a 2-2 draw.

And in this now familiar 'mistaken identity' caper, Keegan managed to clump Billy Bremner, as the pair of them were sent off in the 1974 Charity Shield, played in August. Apparently, Keegan thought he was punching Johnny Giles, the sneaky git who had punched him from behind a few moments earlier. Both left the field, throwing their shirts to the ground, as they railed against the 'injustice' of their dismissals.

In the days when the FA threw the book at those who committed misdemeanours on the pitch, Bremner's book caught him flush, as he was banned for eight games; Keegan's book caught him slightly more than a glancing blow, as he was banned for three games. Both were fined £500.

The country was now perfectly aware of Kevin Keegan's identity.

King Kev finished his majestic spell at Liverpool, winning all the major honours, except the League Cup, signing off with a magnificent display in the European Cup Final, running the best defender in the world, Berti Vogts, ragged. Liverpool won the trophy for the first time in 1977, beating Borussia Monchengladbach 3-1.

But Keegan also knew what he was worth. He knew that the offer of £250k per year at Hamburg would butter more parsnips than the £12.5k per year on offer at Liverpool. And he also had a mission to prove that not every English football export would prove to be a flop. However, those motivations were easily dismissed by the press in 1977, casting Keegan in the role of a greedy villain, gloating triumphantly as Keegan's new team were humiliated 6-0 at Anfield in the European Super Cup.

He stayed three seasons at Hamburg, genuinely struggling to adapt at first; but the arrival of the Zebec-Netzer managerial partnership changed all that in the 1978-79 season, as they won their first-ever Bundesliga. Keegan finished the season as their top-scorer, with 17 goals.

It was at this time, that English fans were denied a proper look at England football's best player. We certainly noted that he looked a better player every time he played for England, but we weren't watching him week in, week out. We were just reading the reports: Kevin Keegan was dominating German football!

And this, too is a crucial part of why we slightly underestimate him: we didn't actually see Kevin Keegan play at his peak. Whilst his fantastic replacement at Liverpool was uprooting trees in the First Division, we didn't see what Keegan was doing at his professional peak, in Germany. He won two *Ballon d'Ors* playing for Hamburg, not Liverpool. He played his best football at Hamburg. Kenny Dalglish came second at the *Ballon d'Ors*, once in 1983.

Eventually Keegan came back to light up English football in 1980. Firstly, part of Southampton's best-ever team, scoring a goal every other game; and then dragging

Newcastle back to the First Division, before retiring from football entirely in 1984.

His international career suffered because England were very unlucky twice in World Cup qualification. His one big tournament, Euro '80, was deemed a failure, after England lost to the host nation and drew with the eventual finalists. An injured back all but ruled him out of the only World Cup he could play in, two years later. But let that not detract from his overall career.

Kevin Keegan was a giant of English football, a colossus of a player at every single team he played. *Machtig Maus* is still English football's greatest ever football export.

Denis Law

The most exciting striker ever

"The boy's a freak. Never did I see a less likely football prospect – weak, puny and bespectacled"
Andy Beattie, Denis Law's first manager at
Huddersfield Town

Denis Law had everything you ever wanted from your superstar striker footballing idol. Razor-sharp reflexes; the instinctiveness of a predator; a gravity-defying leap in the air; a mean, ferocious competitive edge; a flailing of limbs, somehow playing together as a symphony. Take any other player's showreel clip of goals and compare that reel to Denis'. Denis Law wins hands down. Always.

He even patented his own goal celebration – arm in the air, hand clutching his sleeve, finger pointing to the sky.

And those goals came aplenty. Denis Law scored 227 goals in 485 league appearances; 30 goals in 55 appearances for Scotland, a record; 46 in one season for Manchester United, a record. At his peak, he was the dynamic heartbeat at Manchester United, even overshadowing Best and Charlton. There are two statues of him at Old Trafford, too – not the one.

Law's journey to greatness followed a long and slow path, initially. Starting off at Huddersfield in 1955 – staying too long, maybe – he signed for Manchester City for a British record fee in 1960. Before that, he'd had an operation on his eye, which meant he no longer needed to wear glasses. This not only made him a better player, but it gave that extra rush of confidence to the teenager, that never once deserted him on a football field, thereafter.

There had been other offers before the one that took him to City, notably from Liverpool and Manchester United, but he decided to take his career to the next level by choosing City. However, he never really took to City, the way he had taken to Huddersfield, where he had been taken under the fatherly arm of new boss Bill Shankly. And by joining City, he had swapped chasing promotion from the Second Division, for fighting relegation in the First Division. Not the "next level" career move, Denis may have envisaged.

Denis moved to Torino in Italy the following season, lured by the prospect of the extra lira and performance-related bonuses, and to escape the 'maximum wage' salary cap of English football. A striker of his stature would surely earn good money in Italy, and he'd be testing himself against the very best defenders in the world?

Not really, no.

A six-game barren spell brought home the realities of Denis's salary, too heavily reliant on bonuses. He also found the relentless negativity and constant fouling on the pitch too much to deal with. That's even before the paparazzi had followed him all day long, on his day off.

He managed, via a huge struggle, to get himself back to the First Division for the 1962-63 season. Only this time, the red side of Manchester had secured his signature for £115,000. He was also now under the tutelage of fellow-Scot Matt Busby, someone who also shared much in common with Shankly. Busby had been busy rebuilding the team after the ravages of Munich, and United were slowly reasserting themselves. Denis Law was viewed as one of the finishing touches that would precede greatness. They just needed the dash of a little fella from Belfast, and then all would be well.

Denis's first season at Manchester United couldn't have gone much better. He ended the season scoring the first goal in the FA Cup Final against Leicester, as United ran out 3-1 winners. Denis also scored 23 goals in the league, to round off a very successful season that very nearly wasn't. Amidst Denis' successful personal season, United had battled against relegation, and only finished three points above Manchester City, who finished in 21st place. They lost 20 games out of 42 that season.

A second-placed finish behind Liverpool in 1963-64, preceded the first of two Division One titles in three seasons, in 1964-65. Denis was accumulating the goals, and we saw for the first time just what an impact he was having on this United team.

This was probably peak-Law, the time he won a *Ballon d'Or*, the period where his goal-scoring ratio remained at its highest. He was the greatest striker in the land – the energy, the fire, the acrobatics. What a player, he was! We saw all this, because those great teams of the 60s – Liverpool, Leeds, Spurs, Manchester United – were permanently on our TV screens, literally lighting up our lives and living rooms. And that guy – always arguing with everyone; always reffing the game for the referee; always scoring the impossible goal – Denis Law, he was TV's great shining star.

An injured right knee, three times operated upon, plagued his days from 1966-onwards. He missed the United's rightful crowning glory, post-Munich, when they beat Benfica at Wembley in 1968, to win the European Cup.

A slow decline to Denis's career followed, which mirrored the decline at Manchester United. The club's inability to replace the great players that had driven them to past glories, saw a steady descent down the Division One table. There was a cruel inevitability when United were relegated to Division Two at the end of the 1973-74 season. Far crueller, that the new, returning, striker at City had bidden them farewell, with a back-heel at Old Trafford.

This was Denis Law's final act in league football, as he asked to be substituted immediately. An invading mob of United fans cut the game short anyway. Denis later talked about this incident, admitting "I have seldom felt so depressed as I did that weekend."

Denis retired from football completely after the 1974 World Cup Finals in West Germany. He had made 55 appearances for Scotland, scoring a record 30 goals (twice scoring 4 goals in a match), a record he shares with Kenny Dalglish. Despite all his success with Manchester United he still cites being informed about his first cap for Scotland, whilst at Huddersfield in 1958 as his greatest moment. And he still cites beating England 3-2 at Wembley, in 1967, as his most satisfying moment in football.

Denis stayed around football, post-retirement, often as a pundit and as an after-dinner speaker. He always appeared generous with his time and sharing of anecdotes, anytime he appeared on TV. As fans, we love to hear about those stories, the stuff that really went down.

But you would also hear other stories about Denis, how he would give his time to officially open local football pitches and sports centres. About how he would regularly visit a churchgoer at his local Presbyterian church in Altrincham, who spent her last days in a care home. Those visits meant so much to that lady – her hero coming to see her, just for a chat.

But it's the goals – it's the main reason we still love him. Watching Denis Law scoring a goal is still the most glorious sight in football. For a fleeting moment, you get exactly what Danny Blanchflower meant "…the game is about glory, it is about doing things in style and with a flourish".

If you ever want to see what this guy was all about, the flourish, just watch his last ever goal for Scotland against Northern Ireland, during the 1972 Home Internationals. It takes a bit of a root-around on YouTube, but it is so worth the effort.

He's 32, he's past his best. But he still has that magnificent eye for goal. He still knows when to leave the ground – the predator, positioning himself – to make the perfect connection with the ball.

Denis Law was just one glorious football player.

Dave Mackay

A legend at THREE clubs

Studio Anchorman: "So, Dave Mackay, you're in the pundit's chair today. You played for both Spurs and Derby – who are you supporting today?"
Dave Mackay: "I'm a Hearts fan, son."

And that was so true. As the great man said himself "For as long as I can remember all I wanted in my life, nothing else, was to play for Hearts, which is my dream team. And to play for Scotland. I had no ambition for anything else; always Hearts."

What an honour, to play for your hometown team. The team you had always supported, they wanted you to play for them. And they like you, and those fans standing on the same terraces where you used to stand, they love you. One hundred and thirty-five games later, you've won two League Cups, one FA Cup, and a Scottish Championship; you are also the captain of the team. You've even played in a World Cup, over in Sweden in 1958, and you've received the *Scottish Footballer of the Year* award. At the age of 24, you've achieved everything in the game you have set out to achieve.

Your career, Dave Mackay, has barely started.

Down in London, England, Bill Nicholson had recently taken over as the Tottenham Hotspur manager. He had built the nucleus of a decent side, with the likes of Blanchflower, Jones, Smith and White; but so far, the trophies and glory had eluded them. The signing of Dave Mackay for £32,000, in March 1959, would change that forever.

But Nicholson first had to convince Mackay that the challenge of the English First Division was exactly what the homeboy needed, to break that pull of Hearts. Luckily, Mackay listened, and was convinced enough to share Nicholson's ambition; he was also lucky to have a hugely encouraging and supportive wife, Isobel, who convinced her husband that leaving Tynecastle wouldn't be the end of something, but the start of a whole new something else.

And it was this "new something else", that didn't just work out so well for Dave Mackay, but for Spurs, too. Starting from fourth from bottom in the league, when he joined, he became a huge influence – he applied the finishing touches – to Spurs' greatest-ever team. That supremely talented group of players who would win the league championship and FA Cup double in 1960/61, retain the FA Cup in 1962, and then become the first British team to win a European trophy in 1963.

Mackay went on to captain the side to a third FA Cup success in 1967, making 318 appearances and scoring 51 goals. Bare statistics, of course – he also recovered from breaking his leg twice, and had 18 months out of the game, at his peak.

Not only did Mackay make such an enormous contribution on the field but his character was also a major influence in everywhere he went and in everything he did at Spurs. Steve Perryman recalls Mackay's dressing room bravado "Anyone feel like ******* panicking, just give me the ******* ball!".

He was a fantastic leader out on the pitch. Leading by example, relishing a physical battle; his bravery and desire carrying his team-mates and making them want to play like he did. The closest you would get to him today is the Roy Keane of 20-25 years ago. However, he was not just a hard man, he was a really gifted player, with power in both feet, and a great range of passing.

In 1968, as rumours swirled that Dave would be ending his Spurs career to return to Hearts in a player-manager role, Brian Clough, the new manager at second division Derby, nipped in to make the "best signing I ever made". He saw the influence that Mackay could exert on his fledgling team, and even converted Mackay to a sweeper role, to bring the ball from defence to start Derby's attacks, using his incisive passing.

In his first season at Derby, they were promoted to Division 1 as champions. And at the start of the 1970-71 season, they even beat Manchester United in the inaugural Watney's Cup. He left the club in 1971, a year before they became champions of England. But in that season, not only did he lay the foundations for what was to follow, he made 42 appearances in the league for the first time in his career. He was then in his 37th year.

He then, inevitably, stepped into management, at Swindon to begin with. But then came a second calling from Derby in 1973, but it wasn't Cloughie at the end of the phone this time. The Derby board had just called Clough's bluff for the final time, and had sacked him along with Peter Taylor.

Succeeding Clough was always going to be an unenviable task, and the players had now staged a mutiny – Mackay had inherited a desperate situation. However, straight to business, "They are a schoolboys' XI, not men. I am a man and I like dealing with men, not misguided children". Dave Mackay had just taken charge at Derby.

And it took him just 18 months to make his mark, winning the Championship in the 1974-75 season, strengthening the nucleus of the side with the signings of Bruce Rioch and Francis Lee. The glory was over 18 months later, when poor league form led to the Derby board sacking him. Mackay drifted out of management after this, taking up a succession of posts in the Middle East, where he succeeded, and earned the money he could only dream of in the domestic game.

Twenty-two caps for Scotland are a paltry return for his talents. But he wasn't picked for two years, after the anglos were particularly scapegoated after England had beaten Scotland 9-3 at Wembley, in 1961. He also only played the one game, after he had broken his leg twice.

But it's for the leadership and the bravado – at three clubs – for which he will always be remembered. That leadership even takes precedence over him winning League Championships and FA Cups on both sides of the border, and being a Footballer of the Year on both sides of the border. As Roy McFarland said, "Brian and Peter were the people off the pitch that made us a great team and they managed us and coached us, but Mackay was the leader".

He led, not by striking the fear of God into those around him. He led by inspiring his team to play as well as he did, and to be as fearless and determined as he was.

A courageous and fantastic football man, rolled into one.

John McGovern

Captain Invisible

"Who is this McGovern? I have never heard of him.
But he ran the game in the second half"

German legend, Gunter Netzer

Yes, Gunter Netzer said that, after watching John McGovern run "the game in the second half", as Nottingham Forest beat FC Cologne 1-0, in Cologne, to progress to the 1979 European Cup Final.

John McGovern. This guy was so good that Brian Clough signed him four times during his managerial career. He was so good that by the age of 19, he had played in all four divisions of the English football league. He was so, so unbelievably good that he won two Division 1 titles; two League Cups; and two European Cups – and four of those trophies came as the team's captain.

But he was never quite so good that he would earn a full cap playing for Scotland.

The McGovern story begins in Hartlepool, where the family moved from Montrose when John was seven. Tragedy struck the family early on, with John losing his dad at the age of 11. John excelled at the local grammar school, captaining both the rugby and cricket teams. But he played

93

no organised football until the age of 15. A year later, he was playing professional football for Hartlepools United in the Fourth Division, under Brian Clough and Peter Taylor.

But what was it that Clough and Taylor saw in the teenager, that convinced them they had to sign him? What was it that helped make McGovern so successful? What unique game-changing quality did he have in his locker that separated him from the journeymen and also-rans?

The quick answer is: "nothing". John McGovern was your archetypal journeyman, an also-ran, a 'water carrier'. A player's player, a model pro. He would be one of the last picks in a modern-day fantasy football team, his value around the £2.5m mark. He would play every single game in your team, but he would still be your filler; he'd get you 2-3 goals a season from midfield, and probably the same number of assists.

But that tells you nothing about the quality of John McGovern. In his own words he "had a vision of where the ball should go, and I could put it there quickly, with either foot". Brian Clough himself said "He has no pace, no strength, and no great ability. But nobody reads the game better".

And that was McGovern to a tee. He was the midfield irritant who could run all day, and who put his toe in the way of an otherwise inch-perfect pass from a McDermott; the 'blocker', standing in front of a Souness volley; the calming presence, who knew just when to release a pass into the path of a Robertson or a Gemmill. The exact type of player you would barely notice, until your team had been beaten.

His introduction to the professional ranks at Hartlepools preceded a career unimaginable to this young man, who had so recently pulled a football team jersey over his head for the first time. A transfer and two promotions after this introduction, McGovern found himself under the on-field tutelage of Spurs double-winning legend Dave McKay.

The former Spurs skipper was one of many inspired purchases made by Clough and Taylor at Derby County, and it was he that really got the team playing on the pitch. And McGovern was part of that Derby team that somehow inched over the line to seize the Division 1 title in the 1971-72 season. Sadly, McGovern followed Clough to Leeds in 1974, and would suffer for that association – he was isolated from the Leeds team, after making only four appearances. Clough made amends, however, by recruiting him to his new outfit at Nottingham Forest, in March 1975.

A Division 1 title, two League Cups, and two European Cups followed – and it was skipper McGovern who stepped forward to receive those trophies. Never one to bawl out his team-mates, or to go chasing referees, McGovern led by quiet example. Clough admired McGovern's polite demeanour, allied to his steely determination. European football seemed to suit McGovern, too, with European teams and managers seeing and appreciating a 'technician', a master craftsman; a player more like a European player, much less a British player. Clough and Taylor always knew the worth of McGovern the player, to any team they managed.

And it was as the team captain, that John McGovern discarded that cloak of invisibility, to step forward to receive those trophies. Clough knew exactly what he was doing in appointing McGovern as his captain.

As for Scotland, McGovern would have walked the length of a motorway to earn recognition. He was desperately unlucky not to win at least one cap, not to have gone to at least one World Cup. His lone regret, in a career filled with trophies and the utmost respect from those within the game. He loved being told by Franz Beckenbauer, for instance, that "he" had played well in the 1979 European Cup Final against Malmo.

There is much that is unique to John McGovern's playing career, for a player whose position and playing style wasn't unique in the slightest. He fulfilled the least glamorous role in a football team, doing the 'essentials', to stop the other team from dominating possession and scoring goals – he just happened to be one of the best ever in that position.

He also had a very ungainly style of running, a result of a missing muscle in his upper back. He may have needed that muscle to run a yard faster, but it never stopped him running the farthest on a football pitch in every game he played.

His career started very late and it's that snippet, which fascinates. You hear and read of the athlete who suddenly stopped playing football at the age of 15, and discovered that they could run so fast that they could win an Olympic medal five years later. The truth is that there was always an athlete inside the footballer's body.

With football it's different. You rarely start late – every boy in the 50s and 60s wanted to be a footballer, every boy played football. John McGovern just happened to go to the type of school, where his footballing prowess would never have been recognised. It is football's great gain that he did eventually find an outlet for his skill, no matter how late it occurred.

A genuinely great, if hugely unrecognised, player.

Bobby Moore

The best defender you ever did see

"He was one of us. But he wasn't like us"
Jack Charlton

Between 1960 and 1980, you might confidently have identified seven outfield players from the UK, who would have played in a 'World XI', or at least have been part of a 23-man squad. You would definitely have included at least one, maybe two, goalkeepers.

But you might also have challenged the credibility of that claim, if you had watched any episode of *The Big Match Revisited*; particularly if you'd seen Fulham v York City from 1974.

There's Bobby Moore, in all his unmuddied finery, walking into the opposition half with the ball, totally unchallenged. He must have walked between 10 and 15 yards. You might start asking yourself a few questions, such as how he might have coped with today's forwards – constantly pressing defenders back onto their 18-yard line, harrying them when in possession, even tackling them. How would he have coped, and exactly how good was "England's greatest ever defender"?

To counter any of those doubts, you might also have

pored over a few YouTube clips of Bobby Moore's career. Just to remind yourself of the tackles; the triumphs; the glowing testimonials; and his oh-so-cruel and premature passing. And then you might think again about Bobby Moore. And you might just offer your own rightful reappraisal of the iconic footballer that was Bobby Moore. You might also be left nursing one huge and overwhelming lament.

Bobby Moore is West Ham's greatest ever player, and he played more than 600 games for the club during a 16-year tenure, winning the FA Cup in 1963–64 and the Cup Winners' Cup in 1964–65.

Bobby Moore's England career began in 1962, and he won a total of 108 caps for his country, which at the time of his international retirement in 1973, stood as a national record. He also captained England to their sole World Cup victory in 1966.

The bare statistics, of course, which tell us everything and nothing.

What separated Bobby Moore from the mortals, was his actual 'quality'. Rated the best defender in the world by Pele and Beckenbauer – and included in a 'World XI' of the 20th century, voted for by an international panel of judges – he understood absolutely the nature of his role within the team. And we had never seen the like before, not in England, not in the world.

At its most basic level, he was there to sniff out movement of the ball and/ or opposing players, and then to snuff out any possible danger resulting from those movements. It does sound simple, and Bobby Moore made it look ridiculously simple, but that's because Bobby Moore did it so well, that you barely noticed the passage of play you had just seen.

England's best player – the absolute stand-out player – played in defence. That's how good he was. Charlton was great; Banks was outstanding; but your eyes were always drawn to the orchestrator of play in defence. The player, who once he'd made the unflashy tackle, would move the ball on, his aim to switch momentum swiftly.

His close alliance on the field with the other Charlton brother, formed the essential rock around which England's fortunes were built in 1966. The defence conceded just the three goals in six games, the unlikely pairing operating at an almost telepathic level during the tournament. And anyone who made Charlton (J) assume the role of junior partner in any defence, would have had to have been a bit special to earn that level of respect.

Bobby Moore loved the big game – the bigger the occasion, the better he played. His club manager at West Ham, Ron Greenwood, once said that "Bobby is not a bread and butter player. He is made for the biggest occasions." And there was something else we had noticed. He had been a World Cup winning captain at 25, the standout defender in the tournament. But, as the seasons progressed, he was actually getting better.

So that by the time *Mexico '70* had come round, the England captain was playing at his absolute peak, leading a talented England squad that was expected to go close in retaining the Jules Rimet trophy. No matter that the *Bogota Incident* had delayed Moore's arrival in Mexico by four days, he just brushed it aside. It was a down to business, and a World Cup needed to be won again.

"The bigger the occasion, the better he played". There was no bigger game in world football in 1970 than England v Brazil. Drawn together in Group 3, they produced "a game for adults", that to many, would have made a fitting final some two weeks later. Brazil beat England 1-0 in a very tight game; but over the years England fans have forgotten the goal, remembering instead the save from Banks, from Pele. And *that* tackle.

His detractors (yes, there were some), said that he was slow, and that he was not a great header of the ball. But he compensated for his average speed (he wasn't "slow"), with his almost clairvoyant ability to identify a threat, even before the opposition could spot an opening. He knew better than anyone else on the pitch what a danger signal looked like. And as for his heading, Jack Charlton remarked that it was amazing how many times his playing partner would take the ball down on his chest, readily anticipating the flight and angle of a ball in the air.

Watch the 1966 World Cup Final, and see Moore appear in the corner of your screen from nowhere, just as Lothar Emmerich bears down on the England goal. The added and totally expected bonus, is that Moore dispossess him, and still lays the ball off to George Cohen. The bloke was not slow.

And if you really want to see how good Bobby Moore was, just watch that tackle from the Brazil game in 1970.

Jairzinho storms into England's half, angling away from the right touchline. Moore runs in a backwardsy-sideways motion, doing all he can to shepherd the striker away from the danger area. But the skill and speed of the young Brazilian inevitably takes him into just that area. With a matador's precision, Moore goes to ground, and in one movement removes the ball from Jairzinho's toe. Striding forward from the penalty area, he launches England's next attack. The winger who had scorched Cooper in the first-half, to cross the ball for Pele's header that led to Banks' 'Save of the Century', is left a tumbled wreck among the photographers behind the goal.

Moore did something similar, twice more, in tackling Tostao and Pele, during the same match.

And when we found out that Bobby Moore was dying, in February 1993, we refused to believe it. The adonis, the colossus, "our darling Bobby", surely, not him. Not the captain. The best defender we had ever seen. He can't be the first of the gang to die. Not at 51.

Looking at those YouTube clips again, you can still catch yourself shaking your head, mouth wide open, removing a piece of grit from your eye.

A country rightly mourned in his honour.

Bobby Moore will always be remembered as the man who was there at English football's greatest triumph, at the heart of everything surrounding that day. He was also a fantastic ambassador for the world of football. He was just like the other footballers you saw on the telly – but he was so good, and so much better than the others. Above all else, he was England's greatest ever defender.

"Viva Bobby Moore,
Viva Bobby Moore
Viva! Viva! Viva!"

Peter Osgood

The Swaggerer

"He was great in the air and had two great feet. He was quick, skilful and brave. But he didn't have a lot after that"

Tommy Docherty

'The Doc' had also earlier said at a press conference, ahead of the 1965-66 season "I'd like to bet you fellows a year's wages that my centre-forward Peter Osgood could, if he tried a little harder, be England's centre-forward for the 1966 World Cup."

And, therein, was a thread that seemed to occasionally rear its head throughout Osgood's career: "if he tried a little harder".

But that was still some claim to have made by a manager, for whom Osgood had made his debut a mere eight months earlier, against Workington Town in the League Cup. He had scored two goals that night, but he was still put away for that season.

Alright, so it was The Doc who made this outlandish claim, but Osgood still made his mark, even at the age of 18, on the First Division in the 1965-66 season. He played in the league 32 times, scoring seven times. In his first full season, he had made such a name for himself, that he did, indeed, earn a place in Alf Ramsey's initial 40-man squad for the World Cup finals.

The call-up to the full squad of 22 didn't quite happen, but the upward trajectory of Peter Osgood's career seemed an inevitability. He was already endearing himself to the Chelsea faithful, assimilating himself as a fellow 'fancy dan', with his good looks, slim build and a love of London's nightlife.

But he could also play more than a bit. He had even earned an international reputation at this early age, by being named as the best player in the *Little World Cup* youth tournament, despite England losing the final to East Germany. In fact, he was viewed very much as the new style of 60s forward. Quick, skilful, he effortlessly glided past defenders. This was no physical battering ram, relishing one-on-one battles with big defenders. Less the clunky *Jaguar Mark VII*, more the *E-type* model.

However, that upward trajectory came to a crashing halt early next season at Blackpool, in a League Cup tie. Future England captain and team-mate, Emlyn Hughes, broke Osgood's leg, just above the ankle. Osgood took the blame for the break, but he missed Chelsea's run to the FA Cup final that season.

He was never the same player again, and said himself that he had put on two stone in weight, when he returned to the game at the start of the 1967-68 season. "Never the same player", but a different player – a player who had learned to adapt his game, with his new physique. He was certainly a yard slower, and new manager Dave Sexton had now started to play him in midfield.

But by the 1969-70 season, he had regained his place up front with a new strike partner, Ian Hutchinson, a £5,000 buy from non-league Cambridge United. Although this strike partnership has taken on legendary status amongst the older fans, it was very short-lived, lasting about 18 months. And it's no understatement that the arrival of Hutchinson totally revitalised Osgood's career. They hit it off so well together on the field, but also remained great friends and business partners, after they retired from football. Hutchinson's natural spikiness and Osgood's new, tougher, physique made them a real handful for any defence.

They both liked to intimidate defenders, and you can see them both in the 1970 FA Cup Final, not just giving it back to the Leeds bruisers, Charlton and Hunter, but instigating the needle too. Those two marvellous, brutal encounters, ended with Chelsea winning the FA Cup for the first time in their history, with Osgood scoring the equaliser in the replay at Old Trafford (he had also scored in every round of the FA Cup that year).

Osgood's joy was unbounded, however, when he'd discovered that Charlton had walked out of Old Trafford in disgust, refusing to collect his losers' medal! Charlton also admitted that he had failed to pick up Osgood's run for the equaliser, as he had lost concentration and gone looking for Osgood's fellow antagonist, Hutchinson, after he had given Charlton a dead leg.

That season, Ossie had also scored 23 goals in the league, which rightfully earned him a seat on the plane to Mexico for the 1970 World Cup. Once there, he suddenly encountered two problems, however: a. he was competing for one spot alongside Geoff Hurst up front, and the competition was

Franny Lee; Jeff Astle; and Allan Clarke; b. Ramsey wasn't quite taken with the Chelsea centre-forward, not wholly trusting him in a team dynamic.

Ramsey was very much a 'square pegs for square holes' manager, wanting any player worthy of a place in his England team to do plenty of graft, to stop the opposition playing. That said, Ramsey gave all his forwards a chance in Mexico, with Osgood coming on as substitute twice in the group phase. Sadly, to no avail.

The next few seasons saw Osgood's form fluctuate. He only scored five goals in the league in the 1970-71 season, yet somehow his goals in the Cup-Winners' Cup Final against Real Madrid won them the trophy, after a replay. He also scored Chelsea's goal in their loss to Stoke City in the 1972 League Cup Final – always the man for the big occasion.

He drifted away from Chelsea in 1974, after one too many falling outs with Dave Sexton. He came back, briefly, in 1978, a shadow of the player he once was, playing only 10 games. In between, he won another FA Cup with Lawrie McMenemy's Second Division Southampton. That's an easy one to forget.

Two FA Cups and a Cup Winners Cup is a great haul in any player's professional career. But you also get a sense of loss with Peter Osgood. A huge talent on the field, "could have risen right to the top". He was clever enough to reinvent his career, after an injury had threatened to end it. Up to that point, he "was better than Bestie" – Peter's own words, I should add. Others will judge whether he became a better player after that injury in 1966, but he certainly became a different player; a player who had to adapt his skills.

To this day, however, the bloke is still idolised by Chelsea supporters. And it's not just for his achievements on the pitch, that Peter Osgood is so revered. It's because of the way he did it, with the 'swagger' – he made playing football look easy. He would wind up opponents, and he was the ultimate showman. Almost every Chelsea fan you might meet still affects that swagger to this day. He gave them the license to do that, he breathed that outlandish confidence into them.

If he hadn't played football, he would have been that bloke you would have tried to stand next to in The Shed, that uber-cool bloke you went for a pint with after the match and then onto a nightclub 'up West'. He was the ultimate alpha-male, when the term hadn't even been invented. So what that he didn't win as much as his talent deserved. The crown bestowed upon the head of The King of Stamford Bridge still rests easily, some 45 years after Peter Osgood last played football.

And he didn't have to "try a little harder" to achieve that.

Ian Ure

The footballer off the telly

"The greatest centre-half in the world today"
The words of Kenneth Wolstenholme,
during Scotland's 2-1 win against England
at Wembley in 1963

And why not? Ian Ure had played a massive part in Dundee's Scottish Division 1 win the season before, and had been part of the team that had gloriously reached the semi-finals of the European Cup the following season. He had also been part of the Scotland team that had thrashed soon-to-be European Nations' Cup Winners, Spain, in the Bernabeu, 6-2. He had been awarded the *Scottish Player of the Year* at the end of 1962, too.

So, when Ure asked for a transfer in the summer of 1963, why wouldn't Arsenal's manager, ex-England legend and centre-half, Billy Wright have paid £62,500 for the Dundee centre-half, a world record fee for a defender at the time? Billy Wright had been a great player himself, assuming the mantle of 'the greatest centre-half in the world today' in the 1950s. What Billy Wright didn't know about great centre-halves, really wasn't worth knowing about.

And Ian Ure's Arsenal playing career did get off to a reasonable start. Bought primarily to shore up a leaky defence, he was an ever-present in the 1963-64 season. Arsenal conceded five more goals than they had the previous season, but Ure was still settling down into his new surroundings.

However, Ure's future playing problems would occur very abruptly a few weeks into the 1964-65 season, when he attempted a block tackle on Aston Villa's Tony Hateley,

In his own words, he criticised Arsenal for pushing him back too soon, for not allowing sufficient recovery time. He was back playing within six weeks, where it would have been better to have rested for a season. However, he has also admitted to his own impatience, wanting to get back into the first team far too quickly. And he was too quick to swallow a handful of pills – the stuff they gave as tranquilisers to horses – to get himself onto the football pitch.

The consequence of impatience and inadequate medical care were felt for the rest of his career, sadly. Ure battled on, playing until 1972, but he estimates he was only 75 per cent the player he had been with Dundee.

When Bertie Mee replaced Billy Wright in 1966, Ure played regularly that season; but Mee had soon settled on a Neill-McClintock centre-back pairing for the following season. Ure still made 20-odd appearances in both the 1967-68 and 1968-69 seasons, but it was clear that he wasn't a first-choice centre-back.

However, Ure did play in Arsenal's consecutive League Cup Final appearances against Leeds and Swindon Town. Sadly, he left the stadium with a runners-up medal on both occasions, not the treasured winners' 'tankard'. And Arsenal fans still apportion blame, wholly, to Ian Ure for his mix-up with Bob Wilson, that led to Swindon's Roger Smart scoring the opening goal in the 1969 final. In truth, that first goal was a calamity all round for that Arsenal defence, with Wilson and Simpson equally culpable. The ball actually rebounds off Smart's shin, before it rolls into the goal.

As misfortune would have it, the 'Ure-Wilson mix-up' played out almost identically in a league fixture a few weeks later, as Arsenal lost at Highbury 2-1 to champions-elect, Leeds. These were the early days of televised sport, and *The Big Match* had only been on our screens since the start of the 1968-69 season. It was soon looking like that Ian Ure made a mistake in every game he played – his reputation was rapidly being trashed.

And yet – and it is to Ian Ure's great credit – that he had already built up a strong reputation on TV, but via a different route. The BBC had begun the first run of its general knowledge quiz, featuring football teams and their celebrity fans, in 1966. The teams in *Quiz Ball* chose whether to answer four easy questions, three medium questions, two tough questions or one even tougher question to make their way up the electronic scoreboard ('the pitch') and score a goal. Not only did Ian Ure star in the pilot – a 2-1 victory for Arsenal over Nottingham Forest – but also in the final of the first series, Arsenal winning 7-3, this time at the expense of Dunfermline. Here was a footballer, who "knew" things, too.

Ian Ure had become a familiar and knowledgeable face on our screens, but not via the conventional route of today's players, or for the really great players of 60s vintage. It was a great shame that we were still a couple of years away from colour TV, as Ian Ure's magnificent shock of blond hair may well have gained him even more fans. But this was the 60s – and television was new and experimental. Football as a culture was unheard of; its stars had never really been seen before. The idea of mixing TV and football, and mixing it outside the confines of football, seemed to be as good an approach as any at the time.

And you'd hope that for every embittered Arsenal fan unable to forgive Ian Ure for a couple of high profile, televised, mistakes, there would be just as many casual fans and TV viewers, who remembered Ian Ure and Quiz Ball more favourably. Because football is just a game. And no player deserves to take the dog's abuse, just because they made a mistake on a football field, and we all saw it on the telly.

Ian's career then took an unexpected turn, as he became Wilf McGuiness' first signing at Manchester United, for £80,000 – yet another world-record fee for a centre-half! And still with a dodgy knee. He made a further 68 appearances for the 'Red Devils', at a time when they were traversing a new path labelled 'transition'.

He ended his playing days at St Mirren in the 1972-73 season, before briefly managing East Stirling in the 1974-75 season, succeeding some fella' called Ferguson. Ian then took up a career as a social worker, post-football, working in some of Scotland's toughest prisons.

In all, Ian Ure played 378 games of professional football, over a 14-year period in England and Scotland. He played for two of the greatest teams in England, and for a team in Scotland that won its only-ever Championship; he also played in a European Cup semi-final and he played 12 times for Scotland. And he played about 60% of those 378 professional games at 75% effectiveness.

Still going strong, he is a magnificent man and football player. He deserves to still be celebrated and remembered as such.

Ray Kennedy

The Quiet Cog

My personal recollection

As someone born in 1963, my introduction and later love and fascination with football started with George Best. He was probably the most visible and talked about person in the country, and I lapped up all the stories. His European Cups; the great goals in every game; the six goals in one game – he did everything I could possibly want my hero to accomplish.

But soon I became aware that the adults around me were hearing a different narrative surrounding George. I now had uncles teasing me about the sending-offs and suspensions; his arguments with referees; his arguments with his manager because he'd missed training to spend a day with another stunning lady off the telly. I was even hearing that he walked like a woman and he wore a bra. Just how a turncoat 7-year-old should behave, I tired of George's antics and went looking for my new footballing hero.

Looking back now, you would never have said that Ray Kennedy had anything 'boyish' about him. And 54 years later, I still struggle to identify the immediate appeal of Arsenal's "big bloke up front" to this 7-year-old. Maybe it was just that I knew he was 19, and that age was close to

7. And that I didn't know any other footballers as young as 19.

Whatever the reasoning, I was soon asking for an Arsenal shirt and a No.10 to go with it. And then asking my mum to sew the No.10 onto the back of the shirt. It didn't matter that the actual number '10' was black, not white, and that I was "Black-No.10-shamed" at my primary school – I became Ray Kennedy whenever I pulled that shirt over my head.

Indeed, I nearly pulled off the ultimate metamorphosis when I asked my mum and dad to start calling me "Ray". A step too far, maybe, but it was worth the ask. And in a theme that would repeat itself during my formative years, I brazenly admitted that I had switched my football teams because Arsenal were clearly going to be more successful in the 1970-71 football season, than my current team Manchester United.

That Ray Kennedy went on to become one of the most decorated English footballers in history, scaling the great heights of English and European football with both Arsenal and Liverpool, totally vindicated my choice of new footballing hero. A Double-winner, a Fairs Cup winner with Arsenal, he then won five further League Championships, three European Cups, one UEFA Cup and one League Cup, with his next club, Liverpool. He also won 17 England caps. My choice of new footballing hero turned out to be a wise move – I could spot talent a mile away, even at the age of seven.

The circumstances of his arrival at Anfield in 1974, however, were slightly peculiar. Bought as Bill Shankly's last, and record, signing at £200,000, the Liverpool boss had bought Arsenal's striker to provide the depth he thought that Liverpool needed up front. Kennedy had also scored the goal in a 1-0 Arsenal victory at Anfield, that had ultimately ended Liverpool's title push in the 1973-74 season.

But in an off-script moment, that totally threw the world of football, Shankly resigned from football in the summer of 1974. After transforming the club's fortunes during his 15-year reign, it was now left to one of Liverpool's 'Boot Room boys', Bob Paisley, to not only succeed a legend, but to immediately integrate the club's record signing into the team, without the guiding hand of the bloke who had just signed him.

A mixed start to Kennedy's career at Liverpool, resulted in him scoring 10 times in 33 appearances, during the 1974-75 season. By the start of the next season, however, John Toshack had won his place back, partnering Kevin Keegan up front, and Ray Kennedy had lost his place in the team. However, an injury to Peter Cormack in November 1975, gave Paisley an opportunity to slightly tweak his midfield, giving the powerful Kennedy his chance to shine in a new role.

And shine he did. His vision and anticipation, and a knack for scoring goals, made that vital difference to a Liverpool team that were transforming into the giants of the game they would become over the next 15 years. Goals in the title-clincher at Molineux and the first-leg of the UEFA Cup Final against Bruges, coming from 2-0 down, proved his great worth to a team that won two trophies that season.

Over the next five seasons Ray Kennedy missed only five league matches, as Liverpool went on to win three more league titles in 1977, 1979 and 1980. He started to accumulate England caps, too, culminating with playing at the 1980 Euros in Italy. That he only won 17 caps is best explained by the classy presence of West Ham's Trevor Brooking, a rival for the same position on the left side of England's midfield.

You wouldn't always take heed of Kennedy on the pitch. He was the quiet cog; he would go unnoticed. Noticed when he wasn't there, however, when Liverpool had suddenly lost. And just when they needed him, he would pop up with the goal to win a place in a European Cup Final (in 1981). He also popped up to score the crucial second goal in the European Cup Quarter-Final against St Etienne, on *that* night in 1977.

He was the ever-present over the five-year period 1976-81, that established Liverpool's unrivalled greatness in English football. In a midfield that held, at various times, Souness, McDermott, Callaghan, Case, Lee, Heighway, Cormack, Hall and Hughes, Ray Kennedy played in all the games. He was always there to collect the trophies and his winners' medal at the end of the season.

And Ray Kennedy achieved all this, while his body was slowly being overtaken with undiagnosed Parkinson's Disease. This athlete, with his extreme levels of fitness, was gradually losing a battle to maintain those high standards – and the ageing process, and general wear and tear, couldn't fully explain this deterioration.

He gradually drifted away from football, as the effects of Parkinson's took a hold. But not before he was able to win his final League Championship medal in 1982, having joined Swansea City midway through that season. He ended his playing days in non-league football in Northumberland at Ashington, in the 1984-85 season.

When he was formally diagnosed in 1986, Ray was finally able to account for some of the physical difficulties he had noticed, but not shared, in his days at Arsenal and Liverpool. He sometimes had trouble doing up shirt buttons and occasionally suffered from excessive post-match fatigue, but he could never explain this.

The *Professional Footballers' Association* helped financially, and a testimonial match between Liverpool and Arsenal was staged in 1991. One of the brighter parts of Ray's later life, however, was his involvement with the Parkinson's Disease Society, which supports sufferers and raises funds for research into treatments. He proved to be a worthy and noble ambassador.

Shankly compared Ray Kennedy to "Rocky Marciano", when he signed him; Paisley referred to him as "one of Liverpool's greatest players and probably the most underrated". Paisley's description is probably the more accurate, set against the ever-present hyperbole of Shankly. No matter, they both rated him.

Ray Kennedy was a very good footballer – let the medals show that. He was also a great, great man – a magnificent athlete – to have played at the highest level of the most competitive sport for 15 years, with a life-shortening disease that he didn't even know about.

You never like to see your heroes suffer – that image always brings sadness. But above that, you just want your heroes to achieve great things, because that's why you have chosen that person as your hero in the first place. And Ray Kennedy did that. He managed to achieve even greater things by moving to a different club, and he is revered by both clubs, Arsenal and Liverpool, still to this day.

A truly great player of the 1970s and a remarkable athlete, Ray Kennedy, more than that, even, was a very remarkable man. He is still my football hero.